All Is One Love

First published in Great Britain in 2022 by Quacks Books
An imprint of Radius Publishing Limited
7 Grape Lane, York YO1 7HU

A CIP catalogue record for this book is
available from the British Library.

ISBN (Paperback) 978-1-912728-48-0 – Price £9.95
ISBN (eBook) 978-1-912728-49-7 – Price £8.95

Set in twelve point Baskerville. Page size 148mm x 210mm
printed offset on a one hundred gsm chosen for its sustainability.

Reflections upon the transpersonal psychology of time and eternity

Stephen Sayers

Previous Publications

Waiting to the Angel: A Gorton Novel *Ohm Books Publications 2016*
Father Christmas and the Gift of Light   *Radius Publishing 2018*

Acknowledgements

This book has been published with the financial support of the Sessions Book Trust. I thank the Trustees for their generosity. I'm grateful to the editor of *Friends Quarterly* and the Editorial Board of the British Psychological Society for their permission to republish articles from their publications. I'd like to thank my wife, Swea, for providing the wonderful illustrations. Elliot Cohen has my gratitude for his scholarly guidance, unwavering support and for writing the Foreword. My thanks go to Peter Brookesmith, Lorna Marsden, Paul O'Kell and Judy Sagar for their friendship and advice. Claire O'Kell proofread the essays with such judiciousness and has my appreciation and thanks. Finally, Katy Midgley, Jacqueline Coverdale and the directors of Quacks Books in York, deserve a special mention for their patience and professional assistance.

In Memory of Mike Peters

**Hearts starve as well as bodies; give us bread,
but give us roses.**

James Oppenheim 1911

Contents

List Of Illustrations

Acknowledgments

Acknowledgement is due to the following for their permission to reproduce illustrations in this book. References are to plate numbers. Artepics/Alamy Stock Photo, 6, 7; Ian Degnall Computing/Alamy Stock Photo, 8; Heritage Image Partnership Ltd/Alamy Stock Photo, 9; Angelo Hornak/Alamy Stock Photo, 10; Carolyn Jenkins/Alamy Stock Photo, 2; Picade LLC/Alamy Stock Photo, 4; Swea Sayers, 1, 3, 12; Geoff Smith/Alamy Stock Photo, 11. Plate 13, Copyright University of York, not to be produced without permission from the Borthwick Institute.

Foreword

Whether lovingly writing about his hometown of Gorton or engagingly exploring the archetypal origins of Father Christmas, Stephen Sayers is a born storyteller and font of perennial wisdom.

It was Stephen who first brought me to Leeds Beckett University, in 2007, to assist in setting up our innovative Social Psychology degree - one of the very few Psychology degrees in the country that places an emphasis on philosophy and spirituality; actively pursuing deeper questions of meaning, purpose and human potential.

Stephen is one of the unsung heroes of Transpersonal Psychology in the United Kingdom. Quietly working, often unrecognised, behind the scenes - assembling talented individuals (including Steve Taylor and Madeleine Castro) in order to make Leeds Beckett University one of the emerging, leading international centres for Transpersonal Psychological research.

Our initial conversations, now over a decade ago, convinced me of both his depth and breadth of knowledge, while the proceeding years served to demonstrate how all these qualities were tempered with and enhanced by a profound kindness and patience.

In *All is One Love*, Stephen shares his thought-provoking insights gleaned over a lifetime dedicated to learning and teaching. This is not, in stark contrast to the many of the 'Pop Psychology' publications available, a book of easy answers; rather, it is a book that delights in asking all the big questions.

As with Socrates, Stephen similarly appreciates the authentic wisdom of 'not knowing' - never feigning knowledge or self-assurance in the face of life's myriad uncertainties or ambiguities, but rather encountering them head-on, openly and fearlessly.

This is a beautifully written book, quite evidently written by a committed Quaker. I can hear Stephen's voice narrating these chapters, but as importantly, I can also hear his pauses, his silences - the 'expectant waiting' for inspiration and the fruits that follow.

First and foremost, this is a book of meditations, in the confessional vein of Augustine, informed by the Analytical Psychology of Carl Jung, shaped and enchanted by mythological musings.

It is my sincere hope that *All is One Love* becomes a spiritual classic - to be read and studied by Psychologists, Philosophers, Theologians and by anyone who wonders why we wonder why.

Dr Elliot Cohen
Associate Fellow of the British Psychological Society (BPS), Chair of the BPS Transpersonal Psychology Section, Chartered Psychologist, Senior Lecturer in Social Psychology and Interdisciplinary Psychology at Leeds Beckett University.

Preface

In his seminal work of 1980, *Existential Psychotherapy*, Irvin Yalom described what he called the four 'givens of existence' or the inescapable 'ultimate concerns' people face as they live their lives. They were death, freedom, isolation and meaninglessness.[1] Yalom dealt with each of these in turn. He outlined their place in modern life and suggested ways of overcoming the anxiety he claimed these ultimate concerns often create. The essays in this book will refer to Yalom's ultimate concerns as useful ways of thinking about people's lives. However, these concerns will not be considered as separate topics. Instead, they will be discussed freely and in the context of commentaries on the nature of time and eternity.

Time and Eternity

The emphasis upon time and eternity stems from my belief that these forms of perception are basic to human experience. I am convinced that if we are to gain a greater understanding of people, we must address the ways in which they perceive time and eternity because these are channels through which they make sense of everyday life.

Modern people generally perceive time as commonplace and worldly and eternity as rare and other-worldly. Therefore, we might assume that people's accounts of their experiences of time will be more available than their accounts of their experiences of eternity. But this is not necessarily the case. Psychologists have shown how accounts of people's experiences of eternity are sometimes given unwittingly. They can be found in what they say about their experiences of visiting sacred places or listening to music, or falling in love. Descriptions of this kind are where we can find fruitful sources of data for analysis.

This is what I will do here. The essays will use modern psychology and aspects of theology to investigate the relationship between time and eternity and the consequences of that relationship in people's lives. Let me say a little more about this strategy.

Transpersonal Psychology

First of all, the psychology employed in these essays is perhaps closest to the perspective generally known as transpersonal psychology. Transpersonal psychology integrates the models and findings of psychology with various expressions of spiritual insight to explore human subjectivity. In particular, it aims to achieve a highly differentiated understanding of the central importance of spirituality in people's lives. Transpersonal psychology is not the same as the psychology of religion. It does not attempt to make sense of religious behaviour and experience by using psychological theory. It is more ambitious than that. Recently, it has begun to extend its sphere of operation. Its brief now is not simply to integrate psychological with spiritual insights *but to go one step further and produce a theoretical synthesis of those insights.* Transpersonal psychology is setting out to develop the rich synergistic opportunities promised by the fusion of the concepts and methods of modern psychology and spiritual wisdom.

Background

There is a long tradition in psychology of using theological ideas to enrich psychological theory. In the early twentieth century, Sigmund Freud, the founder of psychoanalysis, and Karl Marx, whose influence abounds in modern critical psychology, were both influenced by the Jewish mystical tradition in the construction of their grand theories. Although he was reluctant to admit it, Freud was also influenced by Friedrich Nietzsche. Nietzsche was heavily influenced by Arthur Schopenhauer, the first major philosopher to introduce Buddhist thought into Western philosophy. Nietzsche's influence can also be seen in the work of Carl Gustav Jung. It is also evident in existential and phenomenological psychology, humanistic psychology and transpersonal psychology itself, not to mention each of the several hundred varieties of counselling traditions available today.

Freud, Marx and Nietzsche have sometimes been identified as the founding theorists of much of the present-day social sciences. So it is arguable that at the very heart of their theories and, consequently, at the very heart of modern social sciences, there are ideas imported from theological or at least spiritual sources.

In the late twentieth century, several psychologists built on the founders' theological initiatives. This is especially evident in the work of Jung, who first coined the term transpersonal psychology. Roberto Assagioli developed psychosynthesis, and James Hillman, post-Jungian archetypal psychology, drawing upon spiritual materials. Carl Rogers, formerly of the Union Theological Seminary of New York City, made the link by incorporating theological themes into humanistic psychology. Rogers' influence has been fundamental to several generations of theorists who have, in turn, distinguished themselves by developing humanistic psychology and later, transpersonal psychology. (Abraham Maslow called these the third force of psychology and, the fourth force of psychology respectively. He named psychoanalysis and behavioural psychology as the first and second forces.) [2]

In the twenty-first century, there have been other developments in the field of psychological and theological integration. For example, starting in the late twentieth century and developing in the early twenty-first century, Ken Wilber introduced integral psychology - a mystical synthesis of ideas from around the world intended to chart the way forward for human psychospiritual development.[3] In 2007, Jon James promoted the concept of transcendental phenomenological psychology, based upon the work of Edmund Husserl's earlier work on the experience of transcendental consciousness.[4] In 2014, Manavasi Parthasarathi developed Transcendental Psychology.[5] This perspective was informed by eastern religions and other spiritual sources and sought to elevate the quality of human life. In 2001, Eric Santner used psychoanalysis and Franz Rosenzweig's philosophy to look at monotheism and religious tolerance.[6] In 2015, Paul Axton applied psychoanalysis to examine aspects of Pauline theology to excavate the meaning of sin and salvation.[7] Both Santner and Axton have used the term psychotheology to identify their perspectives.

We can see a similar pattern amongst nineteenth-century theologians who used psychological ideas to enrich their theological theories. For example, the great German theologian Friedrich Schleiermacher imported psychological and sociological ideas into his method of interpreting sacred texts.[8] He believed that to understand the full meaning of a text, one must have some insight into its author's biography as well as the cultural context in which it was written. This method is still used today by hermeneutic scholars. Their principal aim is to interpret texts, not just sacred texts, but any text they choose to study.

In the early twentieth century, Rudolf Otto (whose seminal work, *The Idea of the Holy*, was first translated from German to English by the Quaker, John Harvey) was the first theorist to offer a systematic exploration of altered states of consciousness associated with religious observances.[9] In modern times, his work has been applied successfully to the study of those altered states of consciousness that occur in what might be described as secular circumstances, such as during people's experiences of listening to storytellers, in readers' responses to novels, and even in people's experiences of extreme warfare.

In the late twentieth century, some theologians continued to make links between theology and psychology which were quite specific. For example, Victor White drew upon the Jungian tradition of analytic psychology.[10] Lorna Marsden introduced modern cosmological ideas into her theological writings.[11] Others, such as Matthew Fox,[12] Hans Küng,[13] Paul Tillich[14] (another Union Theological Seminary member) and Don Cupitt,[15] applied themselves to the task of incorporating psychological ideas eclectically in their work. In 1951, well before the publication of *Existential Psychotherapy*, Tillich borrowed the term 'ultimate concern' as a central concept in his theology, albeit with a different meaning from the one first used by Yalom.

These integrative enterprises have demonstrated the theoretical value of the synergy between psychology and theology. Therefore, although transpersonal psychology is not an entirely new venture, it has tended to affirm and accelerate the relationship between psychology and theology by extending their respective spheres of activity. Its primary objective is to sanctify the findings of psychology and to emancipate the insights of theology. Transpersonal psychology does not aspire to be revolutionary in a conventional sense, but it can generate new kinds of data. It is a social scientific perspective that can illuminate people's spiritual lives more fully. It offers social scientists an opportunity to develop a fresh approach to studying human social behaviour and experience and act upon insights that might follow in its wake.

The spiritual insights guiding the analysis in this book will draw upon those provided by various religious and secular sources. However, its main source will be the faith and practice of the Religious Society of Friends, otherwise known as Quakers. Psychological theory and spiritual insights will not be applied evenly to each essay. My purpose will be to explore Yalom's ultimate concerns in ways that seem, to me at least, to be direct natural and unencumbered by social expectations. This will be more evident in some essays than in others.

Eternity and Spiritual Awareness

The essays will demonstrate how an experience of eternity in the present moment can produce a profound changes in people's psychologies. It can trigger an *awakening* of a state of mind that transcends time. Indeed, the experience of an eternal dimension in life can result in an elevated state of mind. I will argue that when this altered state of consciousness occurs, people will be able to experience 'the peace of God, which passeth all understanding' and feel reunited with the source of their being.

An experience of the eternal can create spiritual awareness. People are sometimes alarmed by references to spiritual awareness. They might assume that being spiritually aware involves membership of a religious group or living an impossibly moral life. That is not what is meant here. In my view, spiritual awareness can arise just as readily from *non-religious* as from religious sources. Political affiliation, Freemasonry, humanism, humane atheism, meditation, naturism, yoga, tai chi, mindfulness, and observing or participating in dance, drama, music, the creative arts or athletics can all serve as routes leading to spiritual awareness and an experience of the eternal. The same is true of Taoism, Hinduism, Buddhism, Zoroastrianism, Judaism, Christianity, Islam, Spiritualism, Sikhism or Paganism, or any other religion known to anthropologists. I believe you can just as easily become spiritually aware standing in front of a William Holman Hunt picture in Manchester Art Gallery as you can on your knees in York Minster. Each of these might lead you to an experience of the eternal.

The Eternal Experience

What more can be said about an experience of the eternal? The answer to this question is developed throughout the book. It rests upon the assertion that an eternal experience is nothing less than an incarnation of the divine within the human psyche. Eternal life brings a sense of wholeness and grounds those who experience it. It creates a sense of being anchored by something genuinely authentic in what all too often feels like an inauthentic world. This righteous grounding is solid. It helps people to remain steady in the storms of life. It strengthens their powers of endurance and inspires them to *celebrate* their existence.

At the same time, an experience of the eternal can provide people with a point of perspective from which they can allocate meaning to their everyday lives and make sense of things. Religions throughout the world have tried to teach us this for centuries, but it is something we have so often failed to understand. Throughout history, and certainly, in the present age, there has been a tendency to understand religions in terms of systems of morality - what people should and should not do to fulfil their obligations to a particular faith and thereby secure their soul's destiny. In my view, this is a misunderstanding. Religions are not there to regulate the world; they are there to nourish it. *The purpose of religions is to produce an inspired consciousness, inspired ways of seeing, which translate into inspired ways of being in the world.* When this happens, I believe people find salvation. They will first become fully reconciled to their own nature, and then to the nature of others and to the passage of time.

Definitions

Finally, let me say something about the definitions of time and eternity, which will be employed in the book. The act of definition is not just another scholarly ritual; it is *essential* because the first step in any analysis involves defining what it is the investigator seeks to address. We cannot analyse something until we can identify it, and we cannot identify something unless we have a way of distinguishing it from other things. Definition is the strict mother of analysis.

The concepts of time and eternity are notoriously difficult to define. Definitions of time can be expressed most clearly in prose - in ordinary factual language but more often than not, prose proves to be far too clumsy a medium to capture the idea of eternity. Writers through the ages have done their best to define eternity without achieving much success. The realms of eternity are largely beyond human comprehension, and so it is largely beyond their best efforts to describe it. Nevertheless, it is arguable that we can still perceive eternity at the margins of consciousness. That being so, it is not unreasonable to venture that it can be sketched and analysed. The most successful writers in the field have turned to poetic or mythical language for this purpose. Rather than struggling with factual language, they have expressed what they perceive to be truths about eternity using poetry, myth, metaphor, fable, parables and such like. I recognise the value of this approach, and the essays in this book will make extensive use of figurative rather than factual language in their analyses. I am aware that figurative language will make some of the essays harder to read than others, but I am confident that even a selective reading of the essays will make progression through the book perfectly possible.

In these broadly interlinking essays, I will set out to explain why I have found an understanding of time and eternity to have been such a strong source of direction in my life. I do this hoping that it might help readers gain some additional direction in their own.

The essays 'Transpersonal Psychology' and 'The Quaker Way' are published here for the first time. They appear in the *Appendix* as optional readings for those who wish to know more about transpersonal psychology or Quaker faith and practice. The essay 'Life and Death' is also published here for the first time. All other essays are revised versions of articles first published in *Friends Quarterly* and the *Transpersonal Psychology Review*. 'The Secret of the Rowan Cross' first appeared in *Friends Quarterly*, volume 30, number 8 (October 1997). 'The Ribbon of Time' and 'The Eternal Embrace' were first published in *Friends Quarterly*, volume 31, numbers 4 (October 1998) and 7 (July 1999), respectively. 'The Paradox of Being' was first published in *Friends Quarterly*, volume 34, number 3 (July 2004). 'The Powers of Light and Darkness' was first published in *Friends Quarterly*, issue 1, 2010 and 'Breaking the Chains' in *Friends Quarterly*, issue 2, 2011. 'Flowers of Light' was first published in the *Transpersonal Psychology Review*, volume 14, number 2 (Summer 2011). 'Time and Eternity' was first published in the *Transpersonal Psychology Review*, volume 18, number 1 (Spring 2016).

Stephen Sayers
York 2022

Prologue

If I were asked to identify just one thing that might increase people's enjoyment of life, I would not choose the standard delights of the material world. Instead, I would point to something prophets, poets and philosophers have urged us to do throughout the centuries. I would encourage people to think about the mysteries of time and eternity. Let me say right away that I am all too aware that we live in a world divided by power and conflict and which has been crushed by deep inequalities of wealth, health and opportunities. I realise that an encouragement to think about the alleged mysteries of time and eternity might seem pretentious or plain daft, but I would still stand by it.

I would stand by it because it is my conviction that once we begin to understand the mysteries of time and eternity, we will find what so many of us have been looking for - how to live a better life. Whatever our circumstances, whatever politicians, bankers, bosses, our families, partners, friends and neighbours do or fail to do, whatever it is like to be employed or unemployed, and whatever our health or wealth, our lives can be enriched by an understanding of these mysteries.

Strangely, the way to gain that understanding is anything but a mystery. It is freely available to all of us, and it has been there all the time. We have probably looked at it and dismissed it as gobbledegook or worse. If we did, we did so at our peril. It contains what our ancestors have bequeathed to us and what they felt we should know to endure the things life can throw at us and still find the strength and direction to live a decent life. What, then, is it?

This question can be answered in one word - wisdom. I believe the greatest source of wisdom is to be found in the sacred narratives of the world's religions and myths. When sacred narratives are considered carefully and interpreted in a certain way, they can help us to understand time and eternity and show us how these mysteries work together to create human experience. As we begin to understand what sacred narratives can teach us, they will liberate us, and we will find our lives taking on a kind of dignity. In this state of mind, we will be ready to receive what the scriptures call salvation. And salvation will raise us above the suffering all too many of us find at the centre of temporal life. So let me put my claim to the test and begin to explore the mysteries of time and eternity.

Time

Why do I describe time as a mystery? Well, there are several reasons. First of all, our experience of time can change inexplicably. For example, there are occasions when somehow we can feel *detached* from time. Lovers who have stared into each other's eyes for what seemed to be only a few minutes sometimes find hours have passed. People report that during prayer or meditation, their experiences of time have been changed profoundly. And then, there is my old friend who wanted someone to invent a watch that would reflect accurately his experience of time speeding up on those mornings when he was late for work and then time dragging so slowly once he was there.

In all these cases, people have had unexpected and radical changes in their perceptions of time. When they describe what these were, they often speak of time speeding up or slowing down or experiencing states of mind that appear to be above, below or beyond time.

The mystery of time deepens when we consider the present moment. The moment we are in is a great mystery because it is the meeting place of the past, the present and the future, and yet when you think about it, it is none of these aspects of time. You might say the moment we are in now is the present, but it is not. As soon as you say, 'this is the present,' the first part of that sentence is already in the past. As you finish the sentence, all of it is in the past. You cannot pin the present moment down. It seems to be in a mysterious flux.

The mysterious nature of the present is not only because it represents the meeting point of past, present and future, but also, it *contains and overcomes* them. I can sense readers being bewildered by this statement. It sounds crazy. It might seem less so if we consider how a life bounded and constrained by time - temporal life - can bring suffering and how we might overcome that suffering.

Temporal Life

What does temporal life mean, and why do I think it can bring suffering? Temporal life or living in time means an existence, and that is all it is - an *existence*. It is a state of mind that follows from giving ourselves entirely to the demands of everyday life - getting up, going to work, going through the routines of shopping, using our smartphones, servicing the car, collecting the children, going home and preparing the meals. Can all this really be a source of suffering in peoples' lives? Well, yes, I believe it can. Let me explain why. When we restrict our lives to routine activities, we shut out the wider and deeper experiences of being alive, and we miss so much of who we really are. I know each one of us has pressing responsibilities which we have to carry out. Others in the past have done so for us, and now, it is our turn. I know routines have their uses; I agree with the novelist Joanna Trollope when she writes that we should 'value dullness.' Routines help to regulate our experiences, and, by their very familiarity, they can provide a degree of security. For all these reasons, I do not think routines are problematic in themselves. But I believe they can *become problematic when they are all that there is to our lives.* A life made of endless routine is a kind of servitude. It will be a life where life has gone out of life, and an alienating deadness has entered in. It can be a long and lonely emptiness. Many of us feel like that, and it is tragic that we do. However, we can change this situation and, as we progress, I will do my best to explain how we might set about doing it. First, let me say a little more about what I mean by temporal life and examine the problems that accompany it. What I say might make

4

for uncomfortable reading, but we must consider it to find a way forward.

Temporal life is a way of life regulated by the clock. It is a life driven by purely secular values. There is no lasting sense of direction gained through an experience of things other than material things. By its very nature, it has built-in sorrow. The reason for this is because life in time is experienced *sequentially*. One thing follows another: minutes, hours, days, weeks, months and years, meeting and parting, life and death. For this reason, temporal life involves loss: loss of time, loss of youthfulness, loss of people - our parents, our friends and our lovers. Our children grow up, and we lose them as little ones.

Loss is usually felt as regret, sadness, pain, fear and a desire to return to moments forever beyond our grasp. Sometimes new compensations will arise - new times, new people, new skills, and perhaps, grandchildren. In time, these too will be lost. They, too, will be subject to the same undoing powers of time. If all this were not enough, when we live through repeated losses, we can suffer further losses of the cruellest kind: loss of confidence, loss of self-esteem, loss of interest in ourselves, other people and ultimately, loss of interest in life itself.

Where there is loss - of expectations, people, love, status, jobs or objects, there is often depression. Depression is the painful process of letting go, of weaning ourselves away from something we have invested in psychologically. It is one of the main signs of distress in the modern world, and it is widespread. That is not all, because the expectation of further losses can produce depression's debilitating associate - anxiety. In itself, anxiety is not a problem. It is the psychological equivalent of adrenalin for the body. It prepares us for action in the face of perceived danger. However, when it is constant - night and day - it can be unbearable, and it can affect the way we live to the point where we feel entirely hopeless.

The problem is that when we are so bound up with temporal life, we have only limited opportunities to develop our inner lives. Consequently, we have only limited opportunities to build the psychological resilience necessary to steel ourselves against whatever comes our way. In our schools and increasingly in our universities, those academic subjects that help students to develop courage in the face of difficult intellectual problems have been giving way to less demanding subjects. Less demanding subjects demand little of us. So we give little. We are not put to the test and stretched. In these circumstances, we can be hard put to develop grit, tenacity and confidence, so we are sent out ill-equipped to face the trials of temporal life.

The trials of temporal life can be harsh. When we come up against them, our inadequacies are revealed. We can sense something is lacking, something is not right, and that somehow we are incomplete. Usually, we blame ourselves, those around us, the government, our work, money or the lack of it, and anything else we can think of to account for the way things are. The more determined amongst us will look for ways of making amends and putting things right. More often than not, we will look for temporal things to restore lives that have been depleted by temporal living. This is where the gym comes in, along with new diets, makeovers and going on self-help courses in the hope of gaining understanding and making things better. People will turn to life coaches, social media, spending money, and all those gimmicks advertisers tell us will change our lives, but usually, without achieving much success. If you want to see the results of this way of life, listen to a news channel. On most days, it is a litany of despair. It seems that we are condemned to live profoundly unsatisfactory lives, and I believe this is because we have fixed our gaze outwards. We have been looking in the wrong direction.

What then is the right direction? How can we find a way of coping with the suffering temporal life can bring? Let me suggest something. We might not be able to do much about doing what we have to do in the daily round to earn a living and keep our families together, *but we can change the way we think about it.* We must begin to look at our lives differently. Throughout history, people have found many ways of doing this. For example, they have submitted themselves to different types of disciplined abstinence, such as fasting, celibacy or monastic silence. They have gone on pilgrimages and retreats, and they have used mind-altering drugs. All these methods offer perceptual change, and they can be useful in some circumstances, but they are mostly inappropriate for life in the modern world. However, there are more appropriate ways to create perceptual change. One way is by shifting our gaze from that which is 'out there' to what is 'in here.' We can turn to something within ourselves. We can look for that bit of us that is not regulated by the clock and which is changeless in our lives. In other words, we should embrace eternity and let that steady us in time.

Eternity

Eternity is a mystery. Writers struggle to find the right words to say what it is. I will too, but let me try. Eternity is the source of all things. It is there before time, and it remains there after time. Eternity is absolute presence. It is absolute stillness. Joseph Campbell says of it, 'The eternal cannot change. It's not touched by time. As soon as you have a historical act, a movement, you're in time.'[16] There is no suffering in eternity, but there is suffering in time because time involves movement, movement from this to that. Time involves leaving, and leaving always involves loss, and loss ever bears our suffering. The American sociologist, Robert Bellah, writing about religion in a post-traditional context, makes the point:

> … the deepest truth I have discovered is that if one accepts the loss, if one gives up clinging to what is irretrievably gone, then the nothing which is left is not barren but enormously fruitful … the faith of loss is closer to joy than to despair.[17]

When people are exposed to extreme danger or witness something supernatural, they can experience states of mind that appear to be above, below or beyond time. Their experience is a revelation of eternity. Eternity is what is left when you abandon time. Eternity is where you truly belong. It is your Garden of Eden, where, in time,

8

your soul yearns to return. It is the beginning and the ending of who you are.

Eternal Life

What is eternal life? The question is straightforward enough, but the answer is less so. When I answer it, some people will dismiss what I say. They might think I have given eternal life an irreligious meaning, for I believe eternal life is not some future everlasting life, a hallowed time after death, a Godly infinity. *It is a life that is lived here and now, in the present.* If temporal life is our becoming what we are, then eternal life is *our being who we are*. It is a life lived, directed and nourished by the changeless source of all things. That source is what Mary Magdalene called in her Gnostic Gospel, 'the eternal now.' Others who have gone before us have shown that when life is lit and inspired by eternity, it is possible to live full, useful and joyous lives. In what follows, I will try to demonstrate how we might follow in their footsteps. An experience of the eternal can be ours.

The Paradox Of Being

The tree that would grow to heaven must send its roots to hell.

Friedrich Nietzsche

It must have been in April when I was about sixteen months old. I was sitting in the garden totally absorbed - lost in the joy of play.

There was a strange quality of light. The effects of sun and moving clouds alternated unpredictably to produce lilting extremes of light and shadow. The moment might have passed without ever becoming memorable except that suddenly, I was startled by the cry of a bird. The sky lit up, and for the first time, I realised that I was alone.

I turned to the house, but there was no comfort there. And then I saw my mother's face in an upstairs window. She smiled and waved. The anxiety eased. I looked back at the garden - the limits of my world - in its strange lilting light. But it was true - I was alone. Even though I could see my mother, I was alone.

The thought of it was almost unbearable. Could there be any worse revelation than this? Then after a while, I began to feel something else. It was a kind of joy. In my childish way, I was beginning to understand that whilst my situation was dreadful, it was possible to cope with it and that the very act of coping with it was somehow heroic. That moment was sublime.

What is remarkable about this event is not so much that it happened - the experience of what psychologists call 'infantile separation anxiety' is not unusual - rather, it is because I can still remember the power of it. Indeed, the fact that I can remember it has inclined me to have particular views on life. For example, throughout my professional life, I have never had difficulty accepting that basic proposition of existential psychology which suggests that aloneness is an inevitable and an unavoidable aspect of our lives.

An appreciation of this proposition allows access to a metaphysical truth that can be termed 'the paradox of being.' Its recognition can pave the way to an understanding that beyond existential isolation lies the possibility of an all-embracing communion with the abundance of life. The paradox of being is the subject of this essay. So let us follow the existentialists' proposition a little further and explore its nature. In broad terms, existential psychologists claim that we are born alone, we live alone, and we will most assuredly die alone. The implication is that nothing can save us from the unalterable truth that, ultimately, we are each condemned to existential isolation. There may be times when we are joined in loving relationships or when we can enjoy the company of people and feel a profound sense of belonging. But even in the richness of these moments (the existentialists would argue), the perceptive soul will remain aware of its unrelenting isolation and understand that the great trials of life will have to be faced alone, whatever the circumstances. At the moment of our death, nothing will be able to save us - not the surgeon's skills, or the urgent words or the loving embrace. We will be utterly alone. It will be *our* death, and we will have to bear it alone. To the existentialists, this is the way life is, and any claims to the contrary are simply denials. They are convenient fictions we create in the face of a clear but unpalatable truth.

The proposition is stark enough. Perhaps it is too stark. There is nothing to cover its nakedness. It makes no concessions to human vulnerability. It has the power to disturb us, and yet it has nothing to reassure us. Through its uncompromising claims, we are awakened to the tragedy of our existence.

But maybe this capacity to disturb is one of the most valuable aspects of existential psychology. It might lead us to think about aspects of life that most people would rather not think about. Most of us will do all we can to avoid thinking about them. We have become adepts at flight. Our lives are littered with self-imposed distractions, and we excel in our attention to trivia and the daily round. We delight in our pursuit of superficial fads and sometimes darker fancies, and we co-operate willingly with the endless pap produced by the media. These distractions are our comforts. They serve to banish awful truths from our field of consciousness and render them impotent. But they cannot change these awful truths, and the comfort they bring is but for a time.

Existential psychologists call a life that is dominated by all these self-imposed distractions an 'inauthentic life.' This means a life that is fundamentally influenced by deception rather than by perceived truths. It is a life where value is placed according to the capacity to conceal truth rather than reveal it. And in time, an inauthentic life will become a disordered life because it will be determined by things that do not matter instead of being informed by things that do. In these circumstances, the experience of being alive can only be partial because awareness will be constrained by expedience, and it will not be open to spontaneous perception.

Consequently, inauthentic life will be experienced as though something was lacking or as though something was wrong. In turn, this can produce either an abiding sense of failure or a desire to correct the material world by continually trying to change it. There will also be times when our self-deception fails when our isolation is exposed, and we are suddenly reminded of our aloneness. In other words, with or without self-deception, an inauthentic life will be a life of periodic despair.

Of course, it is possible to relinquish inauthentic life and resume an authentic life. An authentic life requires honesty and the capacity to live courageously. It requires us to abandon our deceptions and acknowledge the inevitability of our aloneness. It does not mean that we will have to accept defeat. On the contrary, once we can say 'if this is the way it is, then so be it' our inclination towards inauthenticity will be arrested.

And once it has been arrested, the paradox of being will be invoked. When we are fully and genuinely reconciled to the idea that we are forever alone, we will experience the full sweetness of being forever conjoined. The one permits the other. Just as darkness is necessary to appreciate light, and a realistic sense of death is necessary for a realistic sense of life, so accepting absolute aloneness is necessary for an appreciation of a revealed sense of togetherness.

In any one of a thousand circumstances, when we find ourselves in accord with other people, we can sometimes experience an unexpected delight. It arises in lovers' sighs and the embrace of the bereaved. It can emerge from the spontaneous making of eye contact following a mutual recognition of irony. It can be found in the smiles that tell of a shared appreciation of a sublime shift of chord in a melody line. Such moments are given to people living inauthentic as well as authentic lives. But in the authentic life, the experience of communion will be especially intense because it is set against a deeper contrary understanding of aloneness. However, because it happens in time, this intensity will pass.

But there is a way an authentic life can lead to an altogether deeper sense of communion. The way has been observed for centuries. It involves taking a metaphysical leap and accepting that our experience of life is not only temporal. In other words, it consists of the recognition that there are aspects of life that are outside of time and are eternal.

Whilst the concepts of time and eternity are not commonly acknowledged, many people will have had an experience of the eternal presence and will understand its nature intuitively. It is a stillness that lies at the centre of the soul and fills us with light when we are in prayer. It is that which is changeless and never ages or dies. It is the very essence of ourselves - the love we offer our beloved people.

The recognition of the eternal aspect of being will lead us to the deepest mysteries of our lives. The eternal presence can help us to appreciate that aloneness is simply an aspect of temporal life. It is only in the field of time where separateness is possible. Such dualities as you and me, here and there, together and alone, are *temporal* dualities. We see things in terms of dualities when we think about the world temporally. But when we reflect upon the world illuminated by the eternal presence - perhaps when we are in a state of prayer or meditation - temporal dualities do not present themselves as opposing qualities; they appear as harmonic aspects of the same thing. The space between self and other people dissolves, and the centred soul finds an abiding sense of union with the created world.

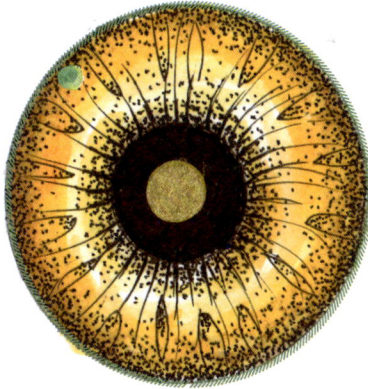

1. Sayers, Representation of Time and Eternity

The relationship between temporal and eternal life is not easy to grasp, but it is possible to articulate it in broad terms. A helpful way to understand and explore the relationship is to imagine a circle that consists of a green line at the circumference and a gold point at the centre. Let the circumference represent time, and the centre represent eternity.

We can see right away that what might appear to be quite different things - the circumference and the centre are just aspects of the same configuration. One defines the other. They complement each other, but it is the centre that is ontologically prior - the centre would still be the centre even if the circumference were to vary in diameter.

Now consider the circumference. A pulse of light travelling around it represents the passage of time. Think of the dualities that this has the potential to create. The movement can be clockwise or anti-clockwise, the pulse can be here or there, or it can be up and descending or down and ascending. The pulse can move quickly or slowly. The orbits the pulse describes can signify past, present and future because the intervals between the orbits can be seen as the last orbit and the present orbit or the present orbit and the next orbit.

Now consider the centre. It is the still point amid the clash of opposites. It is fixed, motionless and immutable. It is the ever-present. It is *Caer Arianrhod* - Polaris and the Silver Wheel of stars that encircle it and which cultures in the northern hemisphere and throughout history have identified as the place of eternity.

Finally, consider the circle in its entirety. It can be a representation of everyday life. Our lives are like the pulse of light travelling around the circumference. During this process, we generally get to know all the dualities of time: the waxing and waning of human lives, our attachments and losses, our pleasure and suffering and our aloneness in the world. But now we might perceive that at the centre of this temporal melange rests the eternal balm, the peace that passes all understanding, the seed with a perfect flower enclosed.

And the flower is God, and God is love, or what Tillich calls, 'the drive towards the unity of the separated.'[18] This is the source of our salvation - our wholeness. When we are mindful of the eternal presence in our lives, we enter into a *participation mystique* with the universe and become psychologically assimilated into the Whole. In authentic life, illuminated by the eternal presence, we find ourselves in union with God.

The state of being 'oned with God' as the author of the *Cloud of Unknowing* has it, has been the primary goal of mystics throughout the generations.[19] Julian of Norwich writes about 'being eternally united to him in love.'[20] Hugh I'Anson Fausset refers to Peter of Alcantara, the fifteenth-century Spanish mystic, and commends his strategy of living life as though 'in the whole creation there was only God and his soul.'[21] Even in modern times, the realisation remains. Carl Gustav Jung refers to a time in his life when in all decisive matters, he was 'no longer among men, but was alone with God … where I was no longer alone, I was outside time.'[22]

There is a profoundly reassuring aspect of the experience of being united with God. It transfigures consciousness. In his work *The Practice of the Presence of God,* Brother Lawrence says of it, 'For my part I keep myself retired with Him in the fund or centre of my soul as much as I can; and while I am so with Him I fear nothing.'[23] And elsewhere, 'I began to live as if there was none but He and I in the world.'[24] See how tenderly this former soldier describes the most elemental of relationships:

My most usual method is this simple attention, and such a general passionate regard to God; to whom I find myself often attached with greater sweetness of delight than that of an infant at the mother's breast: so that if I dare use the expression, I should choose to call this state the bosom of God, for the inexpressible sweetness which I taste and experience there.[25]

The allusion here to a suckled child is seminal. It mythologises the experience and makes it memorable. In the Christian tradition, Jesus taught his followers to think of God as a father. In the Gospel of Thomas, God is described as a mother.[26] These metaphors are not references to gender, but instead, they serve as invocations of something familiar. They connote immediacy as well as a protective and loving dependence. And it is this immediacy that gives the metaphors their power. An invitation to consider time and eternity as a circle with a centre and a circumference has heuristic value, but the image remains abstract and analytic.

However, an invitation to consider the eternal presence as union with the Mother (or the Father) has the power to engage the heart as well as the understanding.

Thomas Merton tells us, 'As soon as you are really alone you are with God.'[27] When we realise our aloneness in time, we must endure the moment courageously until we are led to realise our union with all things in eternity.

So let us seek to know one another in the things which are eternal and live our lives like children in a garden, who have been delivered into the light of the world.

The Eternal Embrace

... in the plane of the eternal, all-knowing, all-seeing, invariable love, there is stillness and waiting and ultimate reconciliation.

Doris Liversidge (from an undated letter to a Friend)

By the time Doris Liversidge died in 1987, she had given us many reasons to remember her. She was benevolent. In her will, she left provision for building a meeting house in Keswick, where she had been a member for over twenty years. She wanted the meeting house to be built in such a way that, during meetings for worship, Friends would be able to look out over the Cumbrian countryside and lift up their eyes 'unto the hills from whence cometh my help.'

She was also compassionate. Most of her life had been devoted to the care of others and especially the care of children. Indeed, she was remarkable in that she had fostered large numbers of children at her home in Pateley Bridge and, in later years, with her sister Elsie, in Cumbria.

But perhaps the most immediate of her qualities was wisdom. When I met Doris shortly before her death, her wisdom was manifest, and it was clear to me that this was the fruit of her spiritual life.

At that time, my children were still small and vulnerable. Like most parents, I would sometimes find myself getting anxious about the future. I felt dismayed about what the poet, Tony Connor, once referred to as 'the wearing-out and dirtying children must suffer to die wise.' But I could find no trace of any such anxiety in Doris. It was as though somehow she still had possession of the children she had fostered. This puzzled me because I could not understand how she could love her foster children so generously and then give them up to the trials of the world. Sometimes she did not know where they were or what had become of them.

I mentioned this to Doris, and her response was entirely unexpected. She said that her children were still with her. At first, I thought she meant that the memories of her foster children were still with her, but she had not meant that at all. She made the point again: whatever the circumstances, she could never be separated from her children. When I confessed that I did not understand, she was reassuring and told me that one day I would.

In all this, Doris had expressed herself with such evident conviction that I was convinced that what she had said was of the greatest importance. I kept her words in mind and reflected upon them from time to time. In due course, understanding came. I began to see that the main reason I had failed to understand Doris initially was that I had been thinking about things temporally. She had been thinking about things *eternally*.

The distinction between time and eternity (and their dynamics, history and myth) is probably beyond any adequate description in prose. However, these terms represent fundamental ideas. Throughout the ages, prophets, theologians and philosophers have found it necessary to struggle with them, to explore the very limits of their experience of being alive.

Of the two, the idea of time is perhaps easier to understand. In modern Western cultures - though not in others - time is generally perceived as a linear progression. It runs at a measured pace from the past to the present and on to the future. (This is analogous to a sequential development of thought. Indeed, thought itself indicates subjectivity in the plane of time.) But what is remarkable about time is how it affects perception because our experience of it leads us to perceive the phenomenal world in terms of countless pairs of opposites. Gregg puts the point comprehensively:

Every aspect of our lives seems to be full of them. Our senses report some of them: hot-cold, hard-soft, sweet-sour, light-dark, sound-silence, fragrance-fetor, vertical-horizontal, rest-motion, winter-summer. Our minds distinguish endless others: truth-error, wisdom-folly, belief-doubt, swift-slow, symmetry-distortion, growth-decay, strong-weak, many-few, cause-effect, change-permanence, creation-destruction, subject-object, attack-defend, willing-reluctance, freedom-necessity, and so on. Our feelings constantly suggest such pairs as like-dislike, pleasure-pain, love-hate, hope-despair. Our moral nature perceives such pairs as good-evil, pride-humility, innocence-guilt, courage-cowardice, respect-contempt. Science describes yet others such as acids and alkalis, positive and negative charges of electricity, magnetic opposite poles, crest and trough of a wave, protons and electrons, analysis and synthesis ... Altogether it is clear that the pair of opposites are an inevitable characteristic of the existence of human beings in this world of space and time.[28]

A life lived primarily in the plane of time will be suffused by ambivalence and perpetual anxiety. This is because the perception of the pairs of opposites will bring alternating experiences of pleasure and pain. For just as hunger implies the possibility of fulfilment, so it is that togetherness suggests the possibility of separation, and life suggests the possibility of death. But whilst a life lived primarily in the plane of time will know anxiety, it will never be entirely without hope. Whatever the circumstances, there always remains the redemptive power of the spirit. Through its intervention, there is the possibility of being returned to eternal calm.

The idea of eternity is harder to understand. But in general terms, eternity is not something that goes on forever, nor does it begin at the end of our time. Rather it exists here and now, and in certain circumstances, we can have a direct experience of it.

For example, an experience of the eternal presence can occur through the contemplation of great art or through prayer, meditation, ritual, dance, drama, music, chanting, or the recitation of, or concentration upon, a narrative. Paul Tillich elaborates all this most eloquently:

For we experience the presence of the eternal in us and in our world here and now. We experience it in moments of silence and in hours of creativity. We experience it in the conflicts of our conscience and in the hours of peace with ourselves, we experience it in the unconditional seriousness of the moral command and in the ecstasy of love. We experience it when we discover a lasting truth and feel the need for a great sacrifice. We experience it in the beauty that life reveals as well as in the demonic darkness of it. We experience it in moments in which we feel: this is a holy place, a holy thing, a holy person, a holy time; it transcends the ordinary experiences ...'[29]

We can find combinations of these activities and their attendant experiences in expressions of worship throughout the world. It is not an accidental association. The activities have a specific purpose. They provide people with a perceptual focus that eliminates attention to the past and the future and absorbs both into an expanded awareness of the present.

In this altered state of being, our minds are freed temporarily from contending anxieties about the future and preoccupations we may have had with the past. A shift occurs in consciousness, inner stillness emerges, and the spirit awakens to the rapture of being alive.

For Quakers, of course, this focus is often provided by silence. Sometimes, in our silent meetings for worship, an experience of the eternal is only vaguely perceptible at the margins of consciousness. At other times, its presence is palpable. In these circumstances, it is possible to have an immediate sense of something that is somehow beyond appearances and upon which everything depends. The eternal presence is widely perceived as being sublime, unchanging, reassuring and charged with the absolute powers of light and darkness.

In the deepest encounters, the eternal is experienced as a sensuous reunion - a return to the source of our own existence. The source is beyond all imagining. It is usually signified by the term, 'God.' Ultimately, everything comes from God and, sooner or later, everything returns to God and is reunited with him.

The eternal presence not only reunites us with God, but it also transcends space generally - it overcomes separateness. Sometimes, in the depths of a gathered meeting, it is possible to sense the mystical union of those present. It is not merely the recognition of a commonality that arises out of a shared purpose or experience. It is born of the quickening realisation that, in the light of eternity, I am you, and you are me, and we are united in the One.

This claim is not new. John's Gospel contains Christ's prayer of supplication for the eternal lives of his disciples, 'That all of them may be one as we are one, Father, just as you are in me and I am in you. Let them be as one as we are one.'[30]

It also occurs elsewhere. For example, Arthur Schopenhauer has addressed the riddle of sacrificial altruism. Why is it, he asks, that when confronted by the sight of someone facing life-threatening danger, we can overcome our instincts for self-preservation and move spontaneously to the rescue? He finds the answer in the profound insight that an experience of danger can sometimes provide. There is something deeper than separateness, the rescued and the rescuer are one. In a metaphysical sense, the death of one means nothing less than the death of the other.

Joseph Campbell has developed this point and has linked it to those who are separated by time. The following account is taken from a conversation with Bill Moyers:

CAMPBELL: ... eternity is not something everlasting. You can have it right here, now, in your experience of your earthly relationships. I've lost friends, as well as my parents. A realization has come to me very, very keenly however, that I haven't lost them. That moment when I was with them has an everlasting quality about it that is now still with me. What it gave me then is still with me, and there's a kind of intimation of immortality in that.

There is a story of the Buddha, who encountered a woman who had just lost her son, and she was in great grief. The Buddha said, 'I suggest that you just ask around to meet somebody who has not lost a treasured child or husband or relative or friend.' Understanding the relationship of mortality to something in you that is transcendent of mortality is a difficult task.

MOYERS: Myths are full of the desire for immortality, are they not?

CAMPBELL: Yes. But when immortality is misunderstood as being an everlasting body, it turns into a clown act, really. On the other hand, when immortality is understood to be identification with that which is of eternity in your own life now, it's something else again.[31]

In this expanded awareness of the present, where we may find communion with God and with each other, we are also nearer to the past and the future than it is ever possible to be. The eternal binds past, present and future together: 'I am Alpha and Omega, the beginning and the ending, saith the Lord, which is and which was, and which is to come, the Almighty.'[32]

Eternity is the source of time, and all time is in eternity. This proximity to the past and the future in the light of eternity contains miraculous possibilities. Events that were once separated by time are reconciled to the present.

Aspects of the past are returned to us. We can have a clear sense of the place of the past in our lives. It is not just remembering or being conscious of detail; it is a powerful sense of its abiding presence, a sense of reconciliation in the indicative mood.

Aspects of the future are also returned to us and are reconciled to the present. The experience of this is qualitatively different from being reconciled to the past. The future is harder to comprehend than the past because we have not yet lived it - we have never experienced it temporarily - and so we cannot always reach for familiar images to articulate our perceptions of it. But it is still possible to sense it, and that sensing can have consequences. This is how prophecy arises. For in the presence of the eternal, the temporal distinction between present and future is weakened, and we can sometimes grasp the future intuitively and express it as prophetic truth. And so it is that prophets emerge from those who have come to live life eternally.

Some Quakers will have no difficulty relating all this to their own experiences. In a gathered meeting, we sink into the radiance of eternity. Here, the past, present and future become one. The living and dead become one. In the silence, we are joined by the ones we have loved. Their presence can be overwhelming. We can feel them with us, fused with our own being in an eternal embrace.

The seventeenth-century Quaker, George Fox, referred to this as 'unity with the creation.' He records in his *Journal* several occasions when he felt himself to be *physically* reunited with those, including the dead, who were separated by time and space.

Quite often, this sense of reunion came upon him when Fox felt 'exceedingly much oppressed' by the troubles of the world. He felt it, for example, shortly after hearing about the death of his mother and when he was reflecting upon the unjust treatment of Quaker prisoners in Derby Gaol.[33]

Arguably, Fox's greatest gift was his extraordinary capability to derive spiritual insight from his own experiences and express that insight to others. In a letter of encouragement to Quakers who were oppressed, Fox drew upon his own experiences of anguish. He observed that the troubles of this world '… are but for a time, and the Truth is without time.'[34]

Perhaps this eternal embrace is what Doris Liversidge meant when she told me her foster children were still with her. For Doris, they might not be present in the plane of time, but they are present in the plane of eternity, where they are forever beyond the trials of the world.

If this is what Doris meant, she must have lived her life in such a way that she was never far from the eternal presence. Indeed, it is not unreasonable to assume that she could do what Meister Eckhart advises us to do - to take into everyday life that link to the eternal we find in the deepest moments of worship.

Thank you, Doris. You were right. There is ultimate reconciliation. And I did live to understand that much and to have sufficient conviction to say so.

The Ribbon Of Time

Meister Eckhart tells us that a helpful way of thinking about God's relationship to our everyday activities is to imagine him in eternity gazing at a historical drama that stretches from the first day of creation to the last day the universe exists. From his advantage point outside of time, he can see everything that was, everything that is and everything that will be. For God, all this happens simultaneously.

It was an inspired vision. Although it is the product of a fourteenth-century imagination, it lends itself easily to our own time and our own generation. Indeed it is probable that, more than any other generation before us, we who are familiar with cinematic technology are better able to visualise the image Eckhart presents.

A consideration of Eckhart's vision can not only help us to appreciate some of the mysteries of time and eternity, but it can also inspire us to meditate fruitfully upon what these aspects of existence mean in our own lives.

It suggests that if past, present and future are simultaneous in eternity, then our tendency to think of existence as a continuous unidirectional movement from the past to the present and on to the future might be mistaken. Eckhart knew this and suggested what that might mean for us by referring to prayer:

Now mark this, and if possible, understand it. In his first eternal glance (if a first glance may be assumed), God saw all things as they would happen, and in that same glance he saw both when and how he would make creatures. He saw the humblest prayer that would be offered, the least good deed that anyone would do, and, moreover, he saw which prayers and worship he would hear. He saw that tomorrow you will call upon him sincerely, desperately pleading with him, and he saw that, not for the first time, he would grant your request: he has granted it already in his eternity, before you ever became a man. Suppose your prayer is foolish or insincere. God will not say no to you tomorrow - he has already said no in his eternity. Thus God, who has seen everything in that first eternal glance, in no way acts from any cause at all, for everything is a foregone conclusion.[35]

Eckhart means that from the perspective of eternity, time can travel in two directions and not just in one. Theorists of the humanities and the social sciences have come up with the same idea. For example, Peter Ouspensky, writing about the symbolism of the tarot, says this of card XIV, 'Temperance (Time)':

An angel in a white robe, touching earth and heaven, appeared. His wings were flame and a radiance of gold was about his head. On his breast he wore the sacred sign of the book of Tarot - a triangle within a square, a point with the triangle; on his forehead the symbol of life and eternity, the circle.

In one hand was a cup of silver, in the other a cup of gold and there flowed between these cups a constant, glistening stream of every colour of the rainbow. But I could not tell from which cup nor into which cup the stream flowed.

In great awe I understood that I was near the ultimate mysteries from which there is no return. I looked upon the angel, upon his symbols, his cups, the rainbow stream between the cups - and my human heart trembled with fear and my human mind shrank with anguish and lack of understanding.

'Yes', said the voice. 'This is a mystery that is revealed at Initiation. 'Initiation' is simply the revealing of this mystery in the soul. The Hermit receives the lantern, the cloak and the staff so that he can bear the light of this mystery.

But you probably came here unprepared. Look then and listen and try to understand, for now understanding is your only salvation. He who approaches the mystery without complete comprehension will be lost.

The name of the angel is Time. The circle on his forehead is the symbol of eternity and life. Each life is a circle which returns to the same point where it began. Death is the return to birth. And from one point to another on the circumference of a circle the distance is always the same, and the further it is from one point, the nearer it will be to the other.

Eternity is the serpent, pursuing its tail, never catching it.

One of the cups the angel holds is the past, the other is the future. The rainbow stream between the cups is the present. You see that it flows both ways.

This is time in its most incomprehensible aspect.

Men think that all flows constantly in one direction. They do not see that everything perpetually meets and that Time is a multitude

2. Pamela Colman Smith,Tarot card XIV Temperance (Time)

of turning circles. Understand this mystery and learn to discern the contrary currents in the rainbow stream of the present ...'[36]

In a conversation with Bill Moyers, Joseph Campbell, the great mythologist, takes the idea a little further:

MOYERS: But what happens to this self-discovery in love when you meet someone else, and you suddenly feel, 'I know that person,' or 'I want to know that person?'

CAMPBELL: That's very mysterious. It's almost as though the future life that you're going to have with that person has already told you. This is the one whom you will have that life with.

MOYERS: Is that something coming from within our inventory of memories that we don't understand and don't recognize? Reaching out and being touched by that person in a way—

CAMPBELL: It's almost as though you were reacting to the future. It's talking to you from what is to be. This has to do with the mystery of time and the transcendence of time. But I think we're touching on a very deep mystery here.[37]

Campbell seems to suggest that the present can be influenced by the future as well as by the past. His suggestion might sound like the stuff of science fiction, but it is not. For many years, philosophers of science have considered it plausible. Michael Dummett,[38] Mary Hesse,[39] John Mackie,[40] Rupert Sheldrake[41] and Sean Carroll[42] have referred to the influence of the future acting upon the present, using terms such as 'backwards causation,' 'retrocausation' or 'back effects' to define it.

The implications of their claim are enormous, and perhaps one could speculate about these indefinitely. There are, however, two points that we can consider here. First, if, as Campbell has just suggested, we can sometimes hear the future talking to us, this process may well explain how prophecy arises. As we have seen, in eternity, past, present and future coincide - they are as one. When we are closest to eternity, perhaps in dreams or prayer or other aspects of devotion, we are closest to appreciating that position God occupies in Eckhart's analogy of the continuum of time. Our being in time becomes fused with our eternal being. We are closer to our past and our future than it is ever possible to be. Here we can gain an immediate impression of both.

Being close to the past is perhaps easier to understand. We have already lived in the past. We can connect names, images, sensations to the experience of its closeness and sense its presence directly. Being close to the future can be experienced just as powerfully, but because we have not yet experienced it in time, the way it appears to us might be harder to pin down. Yet, we will still feel its presence. When this happens, we will experience it as prevision, as a sensing of what is to come. Lorna Marsden expands the point:

The words of the true visionary, belong not to the temporal which is history, but to the eternal …

Are there antennae of the mind which can search out ahead of us regions to which only future generations will openly attain? Foreknowledge of various kinds, telepathy, and the elimination of the barrier of physical distance - these are some of the experiences known to many of us. Today, research into what is known as the paranormal is at last beginning to be acceptable as a possibly

fruitful activity, just as the brilliance of instantaneous calculation without the intermediate steps has been for long acknowledged as occurring.

And these questions lie within the orbit, so to speak, of the relativity of time and space. They serve to accent a probability of truth in the concept of the timeless and the timebound, the bounded and the limitless, the whole and the part, the good and the evil, as inseparable dualities beyond which lies that Whole to which only the mystical vision has so far attained, and that fleetingly. But the act of imagination which conceives such states does not require that they be proved. Such an act of imagination freely passes into that region toward which all prophecy points, and which in itself does not seek authentication, since it appears to reach the threshold of Being itself.[43]

This brings us to the second point. It is a mystery that can send our minds, our sequentially logical (and therefore, our temporal) minds reeling. For if, the consequences of time can travel in *two* directions - if the present can be influenced as much by the future as it is by the past - then it means that sometimes our perceptions of the here and now may reflect more of the what-is-to-come than they do of the what-has-been.

This is a bold claim. It could overturn our assumptions about life. We would have to contend with the possibility that causality can be reversed on the ribbon of time. We are so used to thinking that causes come first, and then they produce effects. Causes are usually thought of as being located in the past or the present, and effects are usually thought of as being located in the present or the future. But now we have to consider the idea that aspects of our present lives may be the effects of causes located in the future.

Our notions of causality may be far more complicated than we have ever imagined. Apart from a myriad of causes located in the past, there may well be whispers from the future, determining the present moment.

So be reassured, young man. You need not think you have been disingenuous about the second love of your life because, somehow, she reminds you of the first. It is not that she is an echo of the love once denied to you. On the contrary, the mystery is this: the first, faltering love of your life was a foreshadowing of that great oceanic love which your second love was to become. Your first love reminded you of the second.

Do not forget, young woman. The stoicism you showed at the death of your first child was given to you by the affirmation of life flowing from the birth of the second.

Be courageous, old man. The death that awaits you is not to be feared. It need not be a lonely ending. It could be a timely celebration required by the birth of your great-great-grandson.

You are blessed, old woman. The serenity at the centre of your heart is not just an expression of the wise innocence that life has bestowed upon you. It is a prescience of that which is to come, nothing less than the bliss of lying in your mother's arms.

And here we arrive at the paradox at the heart of Eckhart's vision. If the prayer is heard before it has been said, if the petition has been granted before the person praying has even thought of it, then it follows that nothing really matters because everything has already been determined in eternity. But the vision also suggests that everything matters. Every act, every word, every silence, every doing and undoing has its consequences in the ribbon of time. Nothing is forgotten.

What are we to make of this paradox? We can begin by acknowledging the idea that paradox is central to the spiritual life. Paradox embodies a union of opposites, and it is, therefore, an expression of the eternal. Paul knew this. In his epistle to the Romans, he suggests that when one loves God - when one is wedded to the eternal - all things, ALL things: past, present and future, work together for good. In short, all things are of God.

So it is that we should never be afraid, we should never give way to despair or arrogance, and we should do what we can to participate heroically in the ribbon of time. And all shall be well.

The Secret Of The Rowan Cross

The secret of the rowan cross was given to me in the summer of 1994. At first, I did not recognise its value. It seemed to be just an old Yorkshire folk-belief, a rustic superstition that had no significance in the modern world.

But now, I realise it does have significance and one which transcends time. It applies as much to life today as it did years ago when it was common knowledge, and, no doubt, its value will remain for years to come.

There is nothing new in what the secret reveals. It is a wisdom that has been declared throughout history and in many cultures around the world. But that does not mean it is a platitude. On the contrary, the fact that it occurs everywhere is a striking indication of the truth it contains.

The full significance of this truth is beyond me, though I can sense something of its power. And power it is, for I believe it can lead those who are mindful of it to experience the miraculous. Before I say more about this, let me explain how I came to find the rowan cross.

It happened during a visit to York Castle Museum. I had been there many times before, and I am familiar - perhaps over-familiar - with its permanent exhibitions. Indeed, I would not have been there at all had it not been for two friends who were in York for the day and who wanted to visit the museum.

During our visit, we found a special exhibition in one of the galleries. It was called 'Stop the Rot' and it showed how objects in the museum's collection are conserved. Usually, this sort of thing would not have interested me and, had I been left to my own devices, I would have gone on to look at something else. But my friends took an interest in it and so, in the spirit of co-operation, I followed their lead and gave the exhibition my full attention.

One part of the exhibition compared decaying objects with similar objects that had been conserved. And this is where I saw the rowan cross.

The conserved version of the cross consisted of two short lengths of rowan branch in the shape of a cross. These were joined at the centre by an iron nail. A notice explained that, in Yorkshire, crosses of this kind were designed to protect people and animals from witches and fairies and other malign influences. The crosses were usually placed over the doors of farm buildings and on the collars of animals. They were to be found throughout the county until the early part of the twentieth century. I warmed to this information immediately. The object and its purpose interested me far more than any details about its conservation.

I was even more interested in the decaying version of the rowan cross. The wood was dehydrated and cracked, and the iron nail was blooming with rust. On one side of the cross was the original exhibition label written in a spidery hand, no doubt by some Victorian antiquarian. Presumably, it was there to indicate that the cross had been collected in pre-modern times.

Whatever the reason, the label contained something quite remarkable. The spidery hand described the cross and its construction. It went on to explain what it had been used for and where it had been found. It said that when making a cross of this kind, it was necessary to 'happen across' the rowan. If the cross was to have the power to protect, the wood it was made from should not have been looked for deliberately; it had to be found accidentally. Then, it could be used. This information stopped me in my tracks. When it had been collected, someone had taken the trouble to say that happening across the rowan was important. It must have been said with sufficient conviction for the collector to make a note of it. The point of happening across was lost on me, but intuitively, I knew it was significant.

Days passed, and the idea of happening across stayed with me. I began to ponder its significance. Was this just a quaint survival of a less enlightened age? Had the instruction to 'happen across' the rowan changed in the telling from one generation to another like a Chinese whisper? Might what appeared on the descriptive label bear no resemblance to the original instruction? The answers to these questions were beyond my knowing, yet somehow, the idea of happening across still seemed to carry power.

Then, I realised that the notion of the importance of happening across something could be found elsewhere. It had a magical significance in certain folk spells. In some spells, it was essential to use blood. But it was often emphasised that for the spell to work, the blood used must be blood 'that had been given' and not blood that had been taken for the purpose. Typically, it had to be blood that had been happened across - the blood of accidents, menstrual blood or the blood of birth.[44]

There are closer examples. I once had the pleasure of meeting a Cornish woodcarver. He would work only with wood 'in the old way' and by that, he meant he would only work with wood that 'had been given by the storm' and contained 'the living sap.' This is a form of happening across. The wood had to be given unpredictably; it should not be intentionally sought after and taken.

'Hag Stones,' or stones that had naturally occurring holes, were once hung above farm buildings, or the thresholds of doors and even around children's necks, to protect them against witches and fairies. Tom Lethbridge, the Cambridge archaeologist, tells us that Hag Stones only had the power to protect if they were found by chance. They had to be happened across.[45]

It is clear then that the magical significance of happening across does not relate solely to making a rowan cross; it might have been a general attitude to folk-life. If it was a general attitude, it has been lost to the modern world, though its value might remain. But what was so important about happening across things? Why was this directive held with such apparent conviction?

I thought about the cross again. The folk who believed the rowan had to be found accidentally were convinced it was of the greatest importance. Happened across rowan was the only rowan that worked, but why? Then it dawned on me. The protective power of found rowan did not relate to the cross itself; it related to the consciousness of the people who were claiming its protection. In other words, the requirement to 'happen across' the rowan had a *psychological* and not a material significance.

A commitment to happening across something produces a different consciousness to that produced by a deliberate seeking. Looking for something suggests a predisposition to take what is required. Happening across something suggests a predisposition to receive what is given.

Looking for something involves an act of volition. The universe becomes the object of the seeker. The act of looking for something is deliberate, instigative and predominantly rational. It implies that the seeker knows what it is he or she is looking for and that, by self-application, the object can be found. Looking for something can produce an orientation to the universe that is highly focused and promotes premeditation, manipulation, and self-reliance.

On the other hand, happening across something involves an act of faith. The recipient becomes the object of the universe. Happening

43

across is spontaneous, serendipitous and predominantly intuitive. The recipient accepts the possibility of unanticipated givings (or takings away) and that he or she can recognise when such events have happened. Happening across something can produce an orientation to the universe that is open and where humility, supplication and awareness of the possible beneficence (and malevolence) of the universe are present.

In short, happening across rowan can feel like something miraculous has happened. It is as though the universe has given the rowan. That feeling can translate easily enough into a belief that *the rowan has otherworldly but benign properties*. This is where a belief in the rowan's power to protect comes from. Those who believed the rowan had the power to protect them *felt* protected. When someone feels protected, their consciousness changes. In this altered state of consciousness, they can find the resilience to face danger. Their confidence grows. Fear gives way to faith, and where there was once dread, dignity arises. It was just rowan that did this for them. A wooden cross had been their way to salvation.

This folk-belief is not so strange, after all. It resonates strongly with the Quaker conviction that ministry should only arise out of silent worship, prompted by God. Often, prepared ministry is not intended by God. It is fashioned by ambition. It is a deliberate seeking for something to say or do. As such, its findings lack the divine *immediacy* of that which is given.

It also resonates with the general Christian conviction that people can achieve spiritual elevation by sacrificing personal will and exercising perfect obedience to the will of God. It was in Gethsemane, where Jesus prayed, 'with a heart … ready to break with grief,' 'Yet not as I will, but as thou wilt' and by so doing, set the supreme example of obedience unto death.[46]

A life based upon the discipline of happening across that which is given is one of a reverential waiting for the divine indication. It could be described as a life based upon the will of God.

This does not mean the faithful should leave every aspect of life to divine providence. If we were to witness a major road traffic accident, it would be folly to wait until we happened across an ambulance. We must seek it out. Much of the world's population would starve if we waited to happen across a solution to the problem of the unequal distribution of the world's resources. We must do what we can to find a solution.

But it does mean we should reflect upon the *apportionment* of both forms of consciousness in our lives to ensure that the exercise of faith is primary. To do otherwise would be to admit that our own efforts are, by themselves, sufficient to achieve salvation. It would be to deny the possibility of the miraculous: the intervention of the divine presence - its unexpected givings and takings away - and that sublime power that pours through a life when it is firmly rooted in eternal grounds.

It has to be said that any attempt to put faith before will is bound to fly in the face of conventional ways of doing things and might attract ridicule. The modern world is preoccupied with temporal concerns. People often assume that success or failure is a result of their own efforts. Because of this, many people feel vulnerable. They live in permanent fear of failure or in the fluctuating hope that one day they will be more than they are. They become anxious about the future and will sacrifice much of the present to try and get future success.

A life based primarily upon the power of faith could be seen as insecure, haphazard and foolhardy. But be assured it is not ineffectual - on the contrary, its potential is revolutionary.

For this is the secret of the rowan cross:

Do not be afraid.

The blessing has
been given.

Walk by faith,
not by sight.

And you will find eternal life.

Life And Death

This mingling of life and death, rising and falling is so strange that we cannot even know where we truly are …

Julian of Norwich

See, how they vanish,
The faces and places with the self which, as it could, loved them,
To become renewed, transfigured, in another pattern.
Sin is Behovely, but
All shall be well, and
All manner of thing shall be well.

T. S. Eliot

At some stage in our lives, most of us will think about life and death. We cannot help it. As we grow up, we begin to wonder where life will take us. There is so much to think about and so many decisions we will have to make. We have to decide about a career, where we are going to live and who we will live with. Then there are haunting questions. How hard will it be? How will I make out? Will I be happy? How long will I have before I die?

From an early age, we learn that pets, neighbours, relatives and friends die. In one way or another, we hear about death all the time. It happens to young and old, but most of us get the impression it happens to the old. At first, it seems reassuringly unrelated to ourselves, but then as we get older, our peers begin to die. Things start to go wrong with us. Our visits to the hospital can become an unwelcome part of our lives, and death presents itself as an ever-present possibility.

In hospital corridors and on the wards, you can witness it first-hand. You hear nurses talking about the new garden centre where you can get coffee and cake. The radio presenter invites listeners to phone in with funny dogs' names, whilst there, on a trolley, is an old woman with yellowed skin. It is the brutal reality beneath the appearance of a normal day.

It is not simply a question of people coming to terms with their mortality. Some people, such as lawyers, medical practitioners and moral philosophers, have a professional responsibility to consider life and death and the boundaries between them. If there are such things as absolute aliveness and absolute deadness, there are still questions to be answered about how and when one becomes the other. It seems that between these absolute states, there are fine shades of being alive and fine shades of being dead. For legal, moral, ethical and practical reasons, someone, somewhere, has to decide what should be regarded as alive and what should be regarded as dead in general terms and in specific cases.

Throughout the ages, theologians of various faiths have also considered what we should make of life and death. Their main concern has been to understand the *significance* of life and death. Theologians of the Abrahamic religions - Judaism, Christianity and Islam, have read in *Genesis* the implication that disobedience to

God's word will result in death.[47] Paul, the founder of Christianity, is explicit about it, 'the wages of sin is death.'[48] In other words, through the assimilation of the Judeo-Christian tradition into western culture, death became known as a punishment for transgression. In the dualistic way of thinking that the Abrahamic religions inherited from Zoroastrianism, where else is there to go from here but to declare that life is good because it is associated with obedience to God's word and that death is bad because it is associated with sin? It is a clear indication that life has to be embraced, and death has to be avoided. It also implies that youth is good because it is full of life and old age is bad because it is close to death.

This is in direct contrast to those sacred narratives that, in their various ways, claim that life and death are adjoined spirits. For example, in the Indus Valley of Northern India, Shiva was seen as the deity of life *and* death. Osiris of the ancient Egyptians oversaw the realms of the dead *and* the creation of new life. The Old Irish god, Dagda, was able to bestow life *and* death upon those around him.

The idea that life and death are, in some way, adjoined spirits also appears in modern times. When Sigmund Freud drew upon Greek mythology to name the life instinct, Eros and the death instinct, Thanatos, he introduced a valuable dialectical dimension into psychoanalytic theory. The relationship between the two instincts was intended to emphasise that although these instincts appear to be separate and opposed, they are set in creative tension. Not only does one define the other, but also, one has the potential to *become* the other. The clash and fusion of each with each creates the course of our psychological lives. In *Beyond the Pleasure Principle*, Freud quotes Arthur Schopenhauer. He wrote, 'If we are to take it as a truth that knows no exception that everything living dies for *internal* reasons - becomes inorganic once again - then we shall be compelled to say that 'the aim of all life is death'...'[49]

Carl Gustav Jung placed the same idea at the heart of his analytic psychology. His use of it came not so much from Greek mythology but the Gnostics of the first four centuries of the Common Era. The Gnostics derived their beliefs from a wide variety of religious and secular sources. In essence, they were committed to the notion that people can escape the world's sufferings through 'gnosis,' through a personal experience of the divine. In the Jung Codex of Gnostic works is the treatise on The Resurrection. It records the Gnostic belief that death is part of life and life is part of death and that the one can transform the other. This idea influenced Jung. He thought life and death were divine aspects of being; they define our lives. In his essay, 'Stages of Life,' he wrote, '... discover in death a goal towards which one can strive, and that shrinking away from it is something unhealthy and abnormal which robs the second half of life its purpose.'[50] Basil Hulme, the late Roman Catholic Cardinal Priest, felt we should teach our children about death and how to die, 'because then, they will learn how to live.' Death is God's last precious gift.

In life, people are generally perceived as the age they have become. This is a young person, this is a middle-aged person, and this is an old person. But death brings life into its fullness and bestows truth to its every stage. Through its blessing, old age can no longer bury maturity, and maturity can no longer hide the child. In death, each becomes an expression of the life that was lived. The beauty, the strength and the wisdom of it are made as one. Its blessing is freely given, and death arrives as a full stop at the end of our sentence.

The transpersonal psychologist, Ken Wilber, takes the idea of stages further. In his case, though, these relate to stages of spiritual development. In his article, 'The Great Chain of Being,' he suggests that life and death are not just necessary aspects of being, but rather, death can be the *supreme accomplishment* of life. He believes that life is a soteriological rehearsal, a preparation for death. Salvation awaits those who can do this well. Those who live in grace will die in grace. At the moment of death, they will achieve a full flowering of spiritual development. He calls this ultimate state 'Spirit' and writes, 'the transcendental nature of Spirit ... surpasses any "worldly" or creaturely or finite things.'[51] Perhaps this is how we should approach the meaning of resurrection.

And we really should consider what resurrection means. We cannot avoid doing so. Accounts of death *and* resurrection can be found in cultures whenever and wherever they occur. Gods such as Ishtar and Osiris in Ancient Egypt, Dionysus, Adonis and Persephone in Ancient Greece, Odin and Baldur in Norse mythology and the Triple Goddess of modern Pagans are all associated with resurrection.

Other examples of dying and rising figures appear elsewhere. In *The White Goddess*, Robert Graves cites the seasonal cycle of life, death and resurrection involving conflict between the Oak King and the Holly King at the summer and winter solstices.[52] A central character in the 14th century chivalric romance of Sir Gawain and the Green Knight is the seasonally executed and then revivified Green Knight. Various figures in Mummers plays, such as Saint George, King Alfred, the Tup and the Slasher, are killed and brought back to life by the Doctor.

The most influential of all the dying and rising figures is Jesus, who has shaped and continues to shape the course of human history. We should not see the fact that Jesus is one of many dying and rising gods as undermining the credibility of what his resurrection represents. Indeed, it only serves to strengthen it. Jung regarded death and resurrection as an archetype, a universally occurring inherited tendency to perceive aspects of life in a certain way. For Jung, Jesus is the embodiment of that archetype; his example is the word made flesh.

According to Jung, archetypes are of major significance in our lives. They link us to all other human beings, whichever culture or historical epoch we find ourselves in. People share the same needs as they pass through the same stages of life. Archetypes organise how we perceive our situation, and they can direct our progress from the cradle to the grave. If we ever become conscious of these archetypal influences, we experience the 'numinous' or something imbued with otherworldly power.[53] By embodying the death and resurrection archetype, Jesus does just that. He bequeaths to the world the possibility of entering the realms of the holy.

Guardians of religions and myths have urged us to understand the meaning of resurrection. Theologians have offered differing accounts of what it means, what we should do to achieve resurrection and what we can expect when we die. In broad terms, these accounts span those who see resurrection as literally true and those who see it as metaphorically true. Some propose a future bodily resurrection, and some propose a future spiritual resurrection. A further distinction exists between those who see resurrection as a spiritual resurrection in the future and those who see it as a spiritual resurrection in the present. Added to these are various accounts of reincarnation, the transmigration of souls and even Friedrich Nietzsche's mind-bending concept of 'the eternal return.' Nietzsche claims we should live our lives as though we were destined to live every moment of them over and over again. He put forward a case for saying this is the wisest thing to do because inevitably, it awaits us all.[54]

We have two choices. We can accept what our religions demand of us, or we can try to think the matter through ourselves. Is it any wonder, so many of us are unsure about what to believe? Is it any wonder, so many of us hope that death is not the end for our loved ones and ourselves?

I know goodhearted people who have thought about resurrection carefully, and they have not been able to accept what is usually meant by that term. In a world that has been permeated by scientific materialism for centuries, the very possibility of resurrection does not seem plausible. At best, they accept it as myth, a metaphor, something understood in terms of this or that meaning. More often than not, though, they see it as wishful thinking, a delusion, something that folks believe as they get older, not because they are wiser, but because they are anxious. The old are usually closer to death than the rest of us. They are often caught between the debilitating polarities of hope and despair. And so often, the fear of death is harder to bear than death itself. They see belief in resurrection as a way of evading the unpalatable truth of people's finality and that of their loved ones.

But then I know others who cope with the threat of death by taking the opposite view entirely. They employ displacement and actively avoid thinking about resurrection altogether. 'I'm far too concerned about what is happening in this life to think about what may or may not happen in the next.' You might think this a noble sentiment, but it is also a psychological defence mechanism in the guise of taking a rational standpoint.

I wish I knew the truth about life, death and resurrection, but I do not. Nor do I believe anyone else knows the truth about these mysteries, no matter how they may wish to argue their case. What I do know is most people are more than capable of reaching their own conclusions in their own ways and in their own time.

And now I must reach my own conclusion. Will this simply add to the store of benign pap which has already been produced? Will it become yet another comforting illusion? Only you can answer that. My conclusion is not offered as a definitive statement; rather, it is an invitation to consider a way of thinking about life and death in a particular way.

There is one tradition that has helped me. Let me ask you to consider it. It is a tradition that addresses life, death and resurrection and one that can be added to any of the other accounts without radically contradicting them. Like much of our modern thinking, it has its roots in ancient Greek philosophy and, in particular, in the work of Aristotle. The notion is first examined in Aristotle's *Politics*, and it has been developed in many ways by theorists who have come after him.[55] What follows is simply one of these ways. It relates to the Greek words for life. In English, there is only one word - life. In Greek, there are two, *Bios* and *Zoe*.

Bios means 'life,' but it means a certain kind of life. *Bios* is particular; it is what every living thing has throughout its lifetime. It is mortal. It comes into being; it lives, and eventually, it dies. It is constrained by time. The words 'biology' and 'biography' are derived from this word.

Zoe also means 'life,' but it means that life which is universal; *it is the stream of life shared by all living things*. As such, it is immortal and not constrained by time. The words 'zoology' and the traditional girls' name, 'Zoe,' are derived from this word.

These two aspects of life are not always rigidly set apart. For example, for so long as there is life on earth, *Zoe* will give rise to *Bios* because *Zoe* is the source of all life. And for so long as there is human life on earth, *Bios* will sometimes give rise to *Zoe* because it is a source of resurrection.

In 1944, C. S. Lewis wrote:

… the difference between Biological life and Spiritual life is so important that I'm going to give them two distinct names. The Biological sort which comes to us through Nature, and which (like everything else in Nature) is always tending to run down and decay so that it can only be kept up by incessant subsidies from Nature in the form of air, water, food etc., is *Bios*. The Spiritual life which is in God from all eternity, and which made the whole natural universe, is *Zoe*. *Bios* has, to be sure, a certain shadowy or symbolic resemblance to *Zoe*: but only the sort of resemblance there is between a photo and a place, or a statue and a man. A man who changed from having *Bios* to having *Zoe* would have gone through as big a change as a statue which changed from being a carved stone to being a real man.

And that is just precisely what Christianity is about. This world is a great sculptor's shop. We are all the statues and there is a rumour going round the shop that some of us are some day going to come to life.[56]

Here, Lewis equates *Bios* with time and *Zoe* with eternity. By so doing, he not only implies the possibility of experiencing *Zoe* once death has ended our *Bios* life, but he also implies the possibility of experiencing *Zoe* in the *Bios* life. Indeed, throughout these pages, it has been a recurring theme that the eternal can be experienced *now* as an altered state of consciousness variously described as grace, dignity, Nirvana, and the like. According to this way of thinking, when eternity is experienced in temporal life, its presence can be life-revivifying. Is this not yet another expression of what resurrection might mean? I would say it is. The supreme example of this event is the death and resurrection of Jesus. And so, it may be said that by his crucifixion, Jesus sacrificed his *Bios* to give humanity the possibility of living a redeemed *Zoe*.

In the *Prologue*, I proposed that our sacred narratives are sources of the acute insights of humanity. Our religions and our myths have evolved over centuries. They carry the wisdom of countless souls. What they have to say has been preserved, tested and enriched by each following generation. It is now offered to us in the modern world. It provides a dramatic way of seeing, a way of experiencing the unimaginable, which is unconsciously compatible with human sensibilities. It is spoken in a language that helps us to understand the trials of life and the sighting of death. It helps us to express ourselves when ordinary language fails. Its words and images can speak to us *now*. They are sources of the renewal of life and the sanctification of death. *And to be sure, they will always lead us to eternity.*

Breaking The Chains

Who speaks of liberty while the human mind is in chains?
Frances Wright 1829
(Feminist, socialist, abolitionist and political and social activist)

When Quakers end their Meetings for Worship, they do so by shaking hands with those around them. It is a universally recognised gesture: a sign of friendship, welcome and agreement that befits

a return to temporal life from the depths of silence. Few people stop to consider the origins of the handshake. It seems such an eminently natural action that it hardly warrants attention. It might come as a surprise then to learn that, in all probability, the handshake has its origins in an ancient Zoroastrian religious ritual.

4. Antiochus I of Commagene Shaking hands with Mithra,
   Bas relief, Gaziantep Museum of Archaeology, Turkey

The first recorded depiction of figures shaking hands is in the Taurus Mountains in south-eastern Turkey. High up on a spur of rock at Nemrud Daği, there is a bas-relief carving of a first-century BCE king, Antiochus I of Commagene, shaking hands with Mithra. Mithra was the Judge of Souls, who was created by Ahura Mazda, a Zoroastrian deity. Shaking hands was not a Greek, a Roman or a Babylonian custom. It was Persian, and in this case, it represented a blessing and an investiture. It was 'kingship descended from heaven.' The handshake served as the transmission of divine power from the supernatural to the natural world. After this time, other ways of greeting such as bowing, kissing and embracing were supplanted by the handshake. This came about when societies that practised Zoroastrianism were assimilated into the Roman Empire. The handshake secured its pre-eminence in the regions occupied by Rome before spreading throughout the rest of the world. Its spread must have happened sometime after the birth of its founder Zarathustra, in about 1300 BCE. But then, the question arises: if the handshake has survived all this time, how much else of Zoroastrian life has made its way into the modern world?

The answer might be unexpected. The principal Zoroastrian bequest to our lives is deep-seated, and yet it is mostly unrecognised; Zoroastrians created our perceptions of morality. Before Zarathustra's time, morality, in so far as it existed, was generally transient. What was good for one person was bad for another. What was seen as good in one set of circumstances was seen as bad in another. There was a tacit acceptance that this was a natural state of affairs. Zarathustra's cosmology offered a radical alternative. He taught that two opposing forces inhabited the cosmos. These were the powers of Ahura Mazda, 'the Wise Lord,' who created the world, humankind and all good things in it and who was Uncreated Eternity. Then there were the powers of Angra Mainyu, who was 'the hostile spirit,' the destroyer of all good things and who was Uncreated Time. These powers were engaged in a perpetual struggle to gain ascendancy. All natural and supernatural events were simply manifestations of their conflict. In their everyday lives, people had to negotiate these influences to secure a place in heaven.

Zarathustra taught that all mortals would be examined after their death to determine how well they had lived their lives. He called it the 'Last Judgement' and likened the process to crossing a narrow bridge led by angels. A spirit called Spenta Manyu judged each soul. Those who had lived their lives devoutly would reach the other side of the bridge and find a paradise known as the 'House of Best Purpose.' But those who had not lived their lives devoutly would fall into a pit of fire known as 'Worst Existence.' In this way, Zarathustra foreshadowed the ideas of righteousness and sin as well as those of heaven and hell.

Here we have the basis of our sense of morality. Zarathustra had proposed that there were things that were absolutely right and things that were absolutely wrong. If one was to enter the House of Best Purpose, one had to side with Ahura Mazda and his values and repudiate Angra Mainyu and his values. One had to adopt a perspective of a conflictual world where light and darkness, life and death, health and sickness and fortune and misfortune were fundamentally and without exception, morally opposed to each other. Where once life and death were seen as brothers, it was now necessary to regard life as inherently good and death as inherently evil. Where once health and sickness were seen as natural processes, it was now necessary to see health as good and sickness as evil. Where fortune and misfortune were once thought of as preordained by gods, it was now necessary to see them as the work of a benign creator and a dangerous destroyer.

This conflictual moral dualism was new to humanity. But its direct simplicity must have been appealing because it soon took hold of the imagination of the peoples who inhabited the Babylonian Empire. The Empire included that part of the world we now call the Holy Land, where Zoroastrian influences informed several books in the *Old Testament*. This is how the Jewish tradition (and later, the Christian and Islamic traditions) inherited an orientation towards conflictual moral dualism.

Jewish writers wrote the book of *Genesis* in the sixth century BCE during their captivity in Babylon, where Zoroastrian duality was prevalent. In the third chapter of *Genesis*, the centrality of a conflictual duality becomes quite evident. It tells us that in the beginning, humanity in the form of Adam and Eve lived in harmony with God and with nature in the garden. If differences existed, they were complementary, and the whole was experienced as Paradise. It was the original state of innocence, the 'as it was in the beginning.' It was peace in the presence of God. Then Adam and Eve did what was forbidden. They ate of the fruit of the tree of the knowledge of good and evil. By so doing, they transgressed a moral imperative and entered a world of duality. They had become cognitive - they were able to think about the mystery of their own lives.[57]

Thought is spatial and sequential, and therefore it is *temporal*. By thinking - by distinguishing - Adam and Eve had entered the field of time, and it is in the field of time where duality occurs. For thinking implies some *thing* thought about. The subject has come to perceive an object. It is the first dimension of duality. Others followed.

In *Genesis*, we find that humanity's sense of duality leads to distinctions being made between male and female, 'they knew that they were naked' and between humanity and God - 'Adam and his wife hid themselves from the presence of the Lord.'[58] Distinctions were also made between humanity and nature in the form of the tempting serpent, and between God and the nature that had hidden them. And following in the wake of Zarathustra, the authors of *Genesis* then introduce a conflictual moral dualism. Adam and Eve came 'to know good and evil.' Through their acquisition of the concept of sin, difference gave way to preference. From that time onwards, this action became good, and that action became evil.

Adam and Eve were expelled from the garden. They were now

destined to experience pain and toil - to suffer the trials of their condition in time, whilst continually yearning to return to that Paradise where, eternally, all is one. And in time, they found the final duality - the memory of a life lived in the bliss of Paradise was opposed by the experience of life lived in suffering outside it.

The influence of Zoroastrian dualism is also evident in the books of *Leviticus* and *Deuteronomy*. The books were written during or just after the Babylonian Exile of the Jews in the sixth and fifth centuries BCE. In *Leviticus*, laws are declared that make distinctions between holy and unholy, or that which is 'clean' and that which is 'unclean.' These developed into distinctions between what should and should not be eaten, what should and should not be worn and above all, which behaviours were permitted and which were not.

In the first century BCE, Gnosticism emerged in the Middle East as a radical alternative to other emerging expressions of Christianity. At the heart of this movement lay a dualism that was also derived from Zoroastrianism. Gnosticism stressed the divisions between light and darkness, knowledge and ignorance and between matter and spirit. But it also expressed the idea that God was not essentially different from humanity and, indeed, that the self and the divine were the same thing. For the Gnostics, self-knowledge was the key to a direct knowledge of God. What mattered was not so much the tension between sin and atonement but the acceptance of Jesus as a spiritual guide. This was necessary to achieve spiritual understanding and the realisation of a full life.

Before this development had occurred, the idea of a conflictual moral dualism had already migrated westwards from its source. It spread to what had by then become Persia and into the nearby regions of the Greek Empire. The diffusion of ideas had happened in the centuries before the Common Era. It was undoubtedly manifest in Pythagoreanism and its sixth century BCE predecessor, Orphism. Pythagoreanism was based upon the ideas of the Greek philosopher, Pythagoras, who had acquired his Zoroastrian principles by being taught by a disciple of Zarathustra, called Zaratus the Chaldean.[59] The work of Pythagoras emphasized the dualistic opposites of an eternal soul and a temporal body. Its eschatology, its views about what happens after death, involved the transmigration of souls. The journey of a soul from one person to another was determined by how well - how righteously - the person had lived his or her life. A strict convention was observed for this purpose, and this was based upon moral absolutism. It was an absolutism that had clear Zoroastrian origins. It divided the good from the evil. Good was light, unity, masculine and limited. Evil was darkness, plurality, feminine and unlimited.[60]

The Pythagorean assimilation of Zoroastrian ideas was to prove crucial. The Pythagoreans had profoundly influenced Plato during his visits to Southern Italy in the fourth century BCE. The tuition he received there became central to his work. Plato's mature philosophy promoted a soul-body duality. It proposed an absolute morality derived from absolute values that were to be defined by an intellectual elite from an eternal source. These values were to lead inevitably to a system of absolute morality. So persuasive were the intellectual and moral expositions of Plato's work that in time it came to shape the entire course of European history. As Alfred North Whitehead observed, 'the safest general characterization of the European philosophical tradition is that it consists of a series of footnotes to Plato.'[61] That philosophical tradition was not confined to academic institutions. Rather it constituted the bedrock of how societies were administered and governed, how people related to each other and how they made sense of life as they lived it. The Magi - the priests of Zoroastrianism - recognised Plato's genius, the man whose work they had helped to create, by making sacrifices to honour him as he lay dying in Athens. So it was that by a beautiful irony, the Magi, the guardians of Zarathustra's ideas in the world, were present at significant events in the two most influential lives in Western culture - the birth of Jesus and the death of Plato.

The effects of all this were compounded by yet another immensely significant development in the Hellenistic world. Pythagorean ideas enjoyed a popular revival in the first century BCE in the form of Neo-Pythagoreanism. Ideas that were carried by the revival into Greek life continued to flourish well into the first century of the Common Era, where they influenced the apostle Paul, the so-called 'architect of Christianity.' Paul had a thorough grounding in the literature of the *Old Testament*. He was familiar with Gnosticism and with the ideas of Plato and Neo-Pythagoreanism.[62] His letters and commentaries combine Plato's dualistic concept of the soul with the Neo-Pythagorean notion of the nature of sin. The result of this fusion informed Paul's moral perspective and the Church he created.

Those Pauline principles were to structure global consciousness for the next two thousand years were predicated upon Zoroastrian conflictual moral dualism. Friedrich Nietzsche was the first to recognise this, though he regarded Paul not just as the Architect of Christianity, but also as 'the genius for hatred, the vision for hatred, the relentless logic of hatred.'[63] As far as Nietzsche was concerned, it was through Paul that the ideas of good and evil, sin and atonement, spiritual life and spiritual death, physical death and resurrection and heaven and hell had gained their historic currency. It was a currency expressed in the language of a distinctive Christian moral dualism. He recognised the conflictual basis of that moral dualism did not come from Paul - it came from Zarathustra and, in Nietzsche's view, it had confounded the world.

Yet when most modern Christians think of Paul, they do so in terms of the persecutor who became the persecuted. They think of the Jew who became the Christian and the man who became the saint. It is deeply counterintuitive to see him as anything other than the practical yet the profoundly spiritual man he was. On the face of it, it sounds like Nietzsche was being irrational and unnecessarily provocative. So let us examine the basis of Nietzsche's claims a little more.

First of all, there can be little doubt that even though he was an impressive classical scholar and a philologist of some standing, Nietzsche was unaware of those modern informed theological opinions that suggest that what we call Paul's work was not necessarily the work of Paul at all. A careful reading of what has been attributed to Paul indicates that more than one person and more than one theology had been at work during their creation. It is arguable that much of what Nietzsche finds at fault with Paul - his separating of God from humanity, his doctrine of judgement, his teachings about guilt and sacrifice[64] and the promise of bodily resurrection after death - were ideas that were probably written into Paul's writings after his death.[65] Elaine Pagels imputes *political* motives to these additions.[66] They represent attempts to exert authority in the emerging Church in the first and second centuries of the Common Era. Nietzsche was referring to 'Paul' rather than to the apostle himself. He blamed the Pauline scriptures for their role in creating human misery. What were his grounds were for doing this?

Nietzsche's seminal book, *Thus Spoke Zarathustra* was designed to present his ideas about the origins of modern morality. The book's central figure, the prophet, Zarathustra, is fictive, though it provided a mouthpiece for Nietzsche's views. The name of the prophet was a literary mannerism. It suggests Nietzsche was being mischievous. From his point of view, a man called Zarathustra invented morality and so it was fitting that a man called Zarathustra should expose it for what it had become - a psychological prison. The prison is our system of moral values. It is a prison in which we are condemned to spend our lives. It determines what we see as right and wrong and how we allocate these meanings to objects, qualities, and events around us. It is, therefore, primary. Our moral philosophy has influenced how we see ourselves and other people, and it provides us with the references we use to regulate our lives. It has contributed to how our society is organised and structured. Our psychological confinement goes unrecognised because its genealogy from Zoroastrian times has been generally forgotten. Therefore, what we regard as moral is all too often seen as somehow natural or self-evidently righteous. Since we are rarely inclined to question these values, we allow them to continue influencing our lives. In effect, we impose them upon ourselves. In his *Journal* of 1823, Ralph Waldo Emerson asked, 'Who hath forged the chains of Wrong & Right, of Opinion & Custom? And must I continue to wear them?' Charles Dickens provided a telling answer to this question in *A Christmas Carol* when he has the ghost Marley say, 'I wear the chain I forged in life. I made it link by link, and yard by yard; I girded it on of my own free will and of my own free will I wore it.'[68] Nietzsche realised this, and he wanted to do something about it.

His concerns lay not only in the *absolute* binary opposites in what had become Christian morality, but he also objected to their content. Since he was a philologist, Nietzsche knew that different cultures set quite a different store by the same things. He understood, for example, that the ancient Jews regarded wrath not so much as a sin but as a virtue. He knew that the ancient Greeks considered hope as a sign of weakness and mercy as an attribute of a fool.

Nietzsche had a point. We are still inclined to adopt an unyielding ethnocentrism and assume that our culture is somehow right and all others are wrong. We exercise a rigid tempocentrism or what C. S. Lewis called 'chronological snobbery' and assume that cultures get more civilised the nearer in time they get to us. So, we should at least address these inclinations and acknowledge the possibility that humanity has no agreed absolute moral values. What is accepted as laudable here is not accepted as laudable there. What was accepted as laudable then might not be laudable now, and what is accepted now might not be accepted in future. We can refer to western culture to demonstrate the point. In a little less than a century, moral attitudes such as militarism, racism, disapproval of homosexuality and feminism have changed from being almost universally desirable to being almost universally undesirable aspects of life. What used to be considered worth dying to uphold are now being consigned to the moral dustbin of history.

Nietzsche's specific objections to the content of Christian morality are beyond the scope of this essay. But it will suffice to record that he felt many of those characteristics we associate with Christianity, such as humility, meekness, and forgiveness, had been derived from a different age and a different set of cultural circumstances from those of our own. He claimed these had come from the time when the Jews had been enslaved in Egypt and, like so many enslaved people throughout history, they had developed a fervent religious outlook and their own sustaining morality. There were two elements to what they did. First, they inverted the values of their masters. What was defined as good by their masters was defined as evil by the slaves. Pride, avarice, envy, wrath, lust, gluttony and sloth - the mark of those who were their masters - were eventually transformed into the seven deadly sins. The second element was that the slaves made moral virtues out of their own survival's cruel necessities. For example, their fear was transformed into the virtue of humility, their impotence became the virtue of meekness, and their inability to fight back became the virtue of forgiveness. Nietzsche felt both elements of this strategy informed a way of being in the world that was effete and restive and which was quite simply harmful to the people who practised them. This included people in the modern world. Lives led according to these principles, were lives conceived and nurtured in a 'slave morality.' They were lives that were partial, inauthentic, self-denying, and impossible to sustain without being overwhelmed by guilt and anxiety. This is the condition Nietzsche claimed we have inherited from Zarathustra. Our lives have been enslaved, and now, the time has come to break the chains that bind us.

Contemporary society has inherited two broad forms of moral dualism. One is absolute moral dualism, and the other is relative moral dualism. Both are problematic. Absolute moral dualism involves the following of a moral code without exception. It usually takes the form of a list of acceptable and proscribed activities. All that the righteous person needs to do is practise one category and keep well away from the other, and then salvation will be assured. There is some comfort in this. People do not have to think too much about things - the way is made clear, except for those who are required to undertake the tricky task of contemplating the semantic twilight zones of moral uncertainty. People know where they stand. They know what is generally considered to be socially acceptable and what is socially unacceptable. Parents can bring up their children to know about right and wrong without ever thinking about what those terms mean.

However, it is sometimes dangerous to challenge this way of life. In general, people do not take kindly to any attempt to question the validity of what might be termed shared core values of 'good' and 'evil' and 'right' and 'wrong.' Such an enterprise can be seen as ignoring the good and condoning evil. It might also be perceived as deeply irresponsible and possibly the product of a deranged mentality. Yet, people dare to do it. Indeed, sooner or later, it is inevitable. What at first seemed straightforward is shown not to be. 'Thou shalt not kill' falters when someone asks if that also applies to plants, malaria-bearing mosquitoes or cancer cells. Does it just apply to human beings? In which case, does that mean it is legitimate to wound or mutilate people as long as they are not killed? These questions are notoriously difficult to address.

The notion that the world is composed of conflicting good and evil forces is sometimes confusing and debilitating to live with. Its main failing is that it helps to perpetuate the idea that good and evil are legitimate descriptive categories. It enables a perception of a moral world divided with simple-minded ease into good and evil elements. Some people feel uncomfortable about this, and their uncertainty can lead to the second position - that of relative moral dualism. William Shakespeare has Hamlet say, 'Why then 'tis none to you; for there is nothing either good or bad, but thinking makes it so: to me it is a prison.' For his own reasons, Nietzsche would agree. Relative moral dualism contains, amongst other things, an attempt to assess the intention or the predisposing circumstances

71

of actions to judge their moral worth. For example, one might argue that whilst it is wrong to kill maliciously, it is acceptable to kill in other circumstances. Perhaps it is permissable when it is done with compassion when someone is in unbearable pain or when one sacrifices one's life for the salvation of others. But if relative moral dualism is adopted, then considerable powers of thought will be required to manoeuvre one's way through all sorts of intentional nuances and predisposing circumstances. Therein lies a problem. Intentional nuances and predisposing circumstances will be infinite, but individual powers of thought are more likely to be finite.

In some cases, it might be too much to ask of us. It can lead to what Peter Berger and Thomas Luckmann have called 'the vertigo of relativity.'[69] Doubt can become endemic. If it does, we risk denying our own perspectives and relying upon those of others. Then the course of our lives will be determined not so much by our reason and conscience but by leading lights in theology, ethics and the social sciences.

Left to our own devices, we might become bewildered and lost. Our lives might become saturated with what the French sociologist, Emile Durkheim, called 'anomie' or that state of confusion and disorientation, which stems from normlessness. This state of being is not conducive to human health and functioning. People cannot live like that. Decisions that affect our lives cannot be made effectively when we live in a state of confusion. It leads to perpetual anxiety and haphazard ways of doing things. But eventually, it can lead to nihilism - a life lived without value - where nothing seems to matter, or where paradoxically, it seems everything might matter, so everything is tolerated. We can see its effects everywhere. We see it in selfishness. We see it in indifference to the feelings of others. We see it in the veneration of violence. And we can see it in crude materialism and in the widespread aesthetic impoverishment that often attends it.

But where there are no clear values, there are no clear grounds for deciding which of conflicting values are to be tolerated or held to be legitimate. This is the main problem with relative moral dualism. If there is a belief that there are no objective moral values that transcend the individual or the culture, then it follows that everyone has a right to a viewpoint, and we have no grounds for criticism. In which case, we will find ourselves tolerating things that should never be tolerated. For example, whatever the intentions or predisposing factors are in its perpetrators, genocide should never be tolerated. It has to be opposed.

We have likely inherited from Zarathustra more than the humane gesture of a handshake. Even allowing for any revolutionary zeal on Nietzsche's part, we might have to concede that our moral principles have been determined by people who lived in a different age and who faced quite different social and cultural circumstances from our own. These moral principles may be incongruent with the present age. Another possibility is that some people's commitment to what they see as God-given moral principles might have become what they think religion is all about. In 1952, Thomas Green wrote:

How far and what ways Friends have come to terms with the latest teaching in physics, biology and psychology, it is difficult for us to say, but I believe that future historians will discern at least a tendency in the thinking of many to replace religion by ethics.[70]

Now, more than half a century later, these words appear to be uncannily prophetic. Perhaps the time has come when we should think again. Admittedly, that is easier said than done. However, once we arrive at a position where we can see that moral codes are problematic social constructions that are all too often turned by words into bonds, we can begin to think anew.

Since the very notion of morality is dual - it divides things into right and wrong and good and evil - it is temporal. Morality deals with life lived in time. Much of our lives are lived in the plane of time, and to that extent, a moral compass is invaluable. Our moral codes provide us with that. Their presence is familiar and reassuring, and many a good and useful life has been lived by their direction. However, a life lived *entirely* in the plane of time and directed *entirely* by dualistic notions of morality can mean a life lived with a restless soul.

Heraclitus knew why. He suggested that not all of our existence is in the plane of time. We have eternal as well as temporal natures. Eternal life is a life lived in an awareness of God. It is not dual. 'To God all things are fair and good and just but people hold some things wrong and some right.'[71] When one lives eternally, one realises the provision of temporality and its dualities and its dependence upon an altogether deeper reality. Joseph Campbell developed this theme when he wrote, '... the experience of eternity right here and now, in all things, whether thought of as good or as evil, is the function of life.'[72] Elsewhere he wrote:

Jesus says, 'Judge not that you may not be judged.' That is to say, put yourself back in the position of Paradise before you thought in terms of good and evil ... One of the problems of life is to live with the realization of both terms, to say, 'I know the centre, and I know that good and evil are simply temporal aberrations and that, in God's view, there is no difference.[73]

Not that this is without its potential dangers. The liberty created by abandoning any general system of morality can sometimes lead to remarkable excesses. We only have to look at what happened in England in the seventeenth century to realise how freedom can lead to extreme self-indulgence. After the execution of Charles I in January 1649, the social order and its expectations were turned upside down. Quakers, Ranters, Muggletonians, Libertines and Adamites, and other non-conformist dissenting groups began to emerge in society. Although these were never discrete groups, they did tend to emphasise the principle that if what people did was in the Spirit, they were free of sin and the law. This often led to inversions of what were then social mores. There were accounts of dissenters engaging in excessive drunkenness, debauchery, public nudity and other activities they claimed were prompted by the spirit of God within, or by the belief that their place in heaven had been assured whatever they did or did not do in this world. So much so that it was necessary to enact The Adultery Act of 1650 and The Blasphemy Act of the same year (under which James

Nayler was tried) to bring such expressions of 'Godliness' under control.

However, the situation in the modern world is hardly the same as in the Commonwealth of England in the seventeenth century. One might argue that the excesses that happened then came from several centuries of oppression being overturned, not by the promptings of love in the hearts of the people. However, the fact that it did happen should serve to make the point that there will always be the possibility of exceptions and falsehoods in the discernment of what is born of the spirit. But these exceptions and falsehoods should never be allowed to obscure those things that are genuine expressions of the 'fire of love' within us. Evelyn Underhill writes, 'The mystics have always insisted, 'Be still, be still, and *know*' is the condition of man's purist and most direct apprehensions of reality.'[74] Meister Eckhart added to this when he wrote:

In the midst of silence there was spoken in me a secret word. But … where is this silence, and where the place in which the word is spoken? As I said just now, it is in the purest part of the soul, in the noblest, in her ground, aye in the very essence of the Soul.[75]

What strength and comfort there is to be gained in the experiences of those who have gone before us. Their strength can be our strength. But how should we gain it? How should we proceed? Well, perhaps we might begin by acknowledging the astonishing influence of the prophet, Zarathustra, in shaping the very nature of the modern world and our participation in it. Judaism,

Christianity, Islam, Manicheanism and the Bahá'í Faith all bear his spirit. Few people have had as much influence on the world as he has. His achievement is manifest. Let his name and his spiritual virility long be remembered.

And we might resolve to uphold our trust in the power of silence. For it is in the silence where we can transcend time and its dualities and where, as Isaac Penington had it, 'there is an ingrafting into Christ.'[76] Paul tells us there are no dualities in Christ, 'neither Jew nor Greek ... neither slave nor free ... no male and female.'[77] In the gathered silence, we are illuminated by the radiance of eternity, where temporal dualities are overcome, where opposites are reconciled and where we find union with God. In this rare light, the promptings of the spirit are made known to us. *This* is where we will receive our direction. Ours is not from this or that convention or from people who claim to have a special relationship with God. Instead, it is from a living, dynamic affiliation with the spirit.

Thomas Green recognised this but also knew it is difficult to take our ingrafting into Christ from the silence and carry it into the 'fever of the modern world' in which we can get caught 'so readily in the swirl of creaturely activities.'[78] We all face this difficulty. Green suggests that we learn from Brother Lawrence, the seventeenth-century French Carmelite monk, whose duties were in the kitchen, to which he had 'a great aversion'[79] and who wrote:

For me the time of action does not differ from the time of prayer, and in the noise and clatter of my kitchen, while several persons are together calling for as many different things, I possess God in as great tranquillity as when upon my knees at the Blessed Sacrament.[80]

Brother Lawrence is here describing eternal life. This is not life after death, but life lived in the eternal presence. The desire to live this way is not new. Eckhart proposed it in the fourteenth century, and indeed, throughout history, countless people who, as Paul would say, have been 'given by the Spirit'[81] have done the same. Nearer our own time, we need to look no further than that Quaker 'Pearl of Faith,' James Nayler, to find an example of someone who lived his life by what he called 'the law in the heart' and not by the laws of convention, and who did so with admirable humanity. This way of life might seem to be an impossibly difficult way to live our lives, but through it, we are offered the gift of liberation.

It is like the carving on the mountain. The hand of God offers investiture, but this time it is an investiture into eternal life. There is nothing to fear. All we have to do is to reach out and accept it. We can do that in our meetings for worship. For in the depths of silence, we return to the sanctuary of Eden. And there, being reconciled to our origins, we are transformed into Adam and enter into a new life - no longer as slaves bound by a moral imperative, but as souls set free by the love of God.

The Powers Of Light And Darkness

Sing and rejoice, ye children of the Day and of the Light; for the Lord is at work in this thick night of darkness that may be felt. And truth doth flourish as the rose ...

George Fox Epistle 227, 1663.

Like all mystical expressions, these beautiful words from an Epistle of George Fox are nearer to poetry than they are to prose. The meaning of the passage is expressed metaphorically, and this can obscure rather than enhance its significance. In the language of psychology, metaphoric expressions are described as 'polysemic.' In other words, the symbols they employ have many and perhaps infinite meanings, some of which will be beyond the author's comprehension. Indeed, Fox would not have been able to grasp the entirety of his own expression, although, no doubt, he would have sensed the power of it.

The use of the metaphors of light and darkness to symbolise the power of God's grace abound in Christian writings. They can also be found in narratives about the spiritual life in other religions, but not always in the same way as they are used in Christianity. In Taoism for example, light and darkness are seen as opposites, but they are opposites set in harmony. One defines the other, each contains an element of the other, and each one is capable of becoming the other. The traditional depiction of this relationship is the Tao, the harmonic duality of the cosmic forces of yin and yang:

5. Symbol of the Tao

Traditionally, yin (moon) is seen as the dark, the passive, receiving, female element of life and yang (sun) is seen as the light, the active, giving, and male element of life. Neither is greater nor lesser than the other. The principles are simply aspects of the same thing. Both contain the seeds of each other. Both are necessary to make life possible, and a graceful human life can only be lived through their union and harmony.

Similar uses of the metaphors occur elsewhere. In the Hindu religion, for example, Brama, the creator of all, has a triumvirate of lesser gods who work out his purposes in the universe. These are Vishnu, who is associated with light and creation, and Shiva, who is associated with darkness and the destruction of evil (and who is, therefore, paradoxically, a force for creation) and Brama, who keeps the activities of the other two gods in harmony.

In the Middle East, a Mesopotamian creation myth dating from at least the third century BCE is recorded in the fourth tablet of the *Epic of Creation* that was written in the fifth century BCE. It tells how Marduk, son of Ea and god of light, achieved a momentous victory over Tiamat, the mother of chaos and confusion, who was darkness and who had 'conceived evil in her heart.' Marduk turned the victory to the good by splitting her open 'like a flat fish into two halves' and making one of the halves into a covering for heaven.

But it was Zarathustra, the founder of Zoroastrianism, who used the metaphors of light and darkness to greatest effect. Zarathustra was familiar with how the metaphors were used in Hinduism. This was because at the time of his birth in about 1300 BCE, the region where he was born, Bactria, in Eastern Iran, had shared cultural characteristics with Afghanistan, which was then mostly Hindu. (He would also have known about the Mesopotamian *Epic of Creation*, because Mesopotamia was contiguous with Bactria.) Zarathustra modified the Hindu usage. He simplified it but retained its harmonic dualism and the idea that the universe was inhabited and made manifest by the powers of light and darkness, which he described as twin brothers. The power of light was personified as Ahura Mazda, 'the Wise Lord,' and the power of darkness was personified as Angra Mainyu, 'the Lie.' So that according to Zarathustra, Ahura Mazda brought the day, and Angra Mainyu brought the night. Ahura Mazda made winter turn into summer, and Angra Mainyu made summer turn into winter. Ahura Mazda made the seed germinate and grow, and Angra Mainyu made the vegetation produced turn brown and die.

After Zarathustra's death, the ideas he had generated continued to evolve. But significantly, the original harmonic dualism between light and darkness was abandoned, and in its place, the earlier Mesopotamian motif was adopted. The narrative was transformed into one embodying a *conflictual* dualism - a dualism based upon the clash of irreconcilable opposites. Ahura Mazda came to be seen as the creator of all things, and Angra Mainyu, 'who is all death' came to be seen as the destroyer of all things. The convulsions of the universe and the course of history were regarded as the products of an endless struggle between these two cosmic powers. But the most crucial battleground on which they met and fought for supremacy was in the spiritual, moral and ethical lives of people.

These figures became prevalent in the region. Ahura Mazda came to represent all that was good, and Angra Mainyu came to represent all that was evil. It was understood that the wise soul should live by the qualities and aspirations of Ahura Mazda and oppose those of Angra Mainyu. This simple dualism seemed to strike a chord with those who heard about it. It could help them to make sense of their experience of life. Fortune and misfortune were reflctions of the cosmic battle being waged. So compelling was this imagery that the conflict between Ahura Mazda and Angra Mainyu were to influence later ideas about God and Satan in the Abrahamic religions of Judaism, Christianity and Islam.

Ideas about light and darkness, good and evil, and how they were in conflict with each other began to spread. Jewish thinkers came into contact with them in the sixth century BCE, when they were converting some of their orthodox religious texts into the later books of the *Old Testament*. At that time, the Persian Empire dominated most of what we now call the Middle East and some of the key ideas of Zoroastrianism had become influential. Conflictual dualism and its offspring, moral absolutism, began to emerge as central guiding concepts in the Judaic worldview. In the first few lines of *Genesis*, we can find the Zoroastrian influence, 'God said, Let there be light: and there was light. And God saw the light, that it was good: and God divided the light from the darkness.' These lines introduce the metaphors of light and darkness in terms of moral opposites and have served to structure the perceptions of people around the world to the present day.

One of the ways this happened was through its appearance in Essene teachings. In 1947, a sacred Essene text titled, *Scroll of the War of the Sons of Light Against The Sons of Darkness* was discovered amongst the Dead Sea Scrolls. It told of the Sons of Light, who were the Essenes, and the Sons of Darkness, who were probably the Romans and others, who had 'violated the precept.' These were engaged in a perpetual war. The Prince of Light clashed eternally with the Prince of Darkness. It was a war of good against evil that had both cosmic and historical consequences. As the battle raged, it produced natural and supernatural events. But the effects of all this - both cosmic and historical - were felt most acutely in the human heart.

From a modern standpoint, the significance of Essene cosmology might easily be dismissed as the strange imaginings of an obscure Jewish sect. However, several recent scholars have suggested that both John the Baptist and Jesus had Essenic roots or at least, Essenic leanings and that their contributions to what would become a global Christianity would guarantee that Essenic influences would survive.[82]

In the *New Testament*, the use of the Zoroastrian metaphors of light and darkness abound, but nowhere do they appear as clearly as they do in the letters of Paul. His use of the metaphors is seminal. Through the 'Mother Church' he founded, Paul conveyed Zarathustra's conflictual dualism directly to modern global consciousness. Witness, for example, how Paul foreshadowed George Fox when he wrote to the Thessalonians, 'We are all the children of light, and the children of the day: we are not of the night, nor of darkness.'[83] And to the Romans, 'let us therefore cast off the works of darkness, and let us put on the armour of light.'[84]

Writing in the second century CE, John takes up the tradition and consolidates it:

And this is the condemnation, that light is come into the world, and men loved darkness rather than light, because their deeds were evil. For every one that doeth evil hateth the light, lest his deeds should be reproved. But he that doeth truth cometh to the light, that his deeds may be made manifest, that they are wrought in God.[85]

In the following century, the followers of Mani, the Persian prophet, founded an unorthodox Gnostic religion that has come to be known as Manichaeism. Manichaeism is not the force it was and is probably now extinct, but once it was of enormous influence in the Middle East. Its theology travelled via the silk route to China, and in due course, it reached the West, where for a time it was influential.[86] A basic tenet of Manichaeism was the central dualistic Zoroastrian metaphor. The cosmos was described as a battleground for the powers of light, which were good, and the powers of darkness, which were evil. Souls were seen as sparks of light that inhabited the darkness of the material world. A Chinese Manichean scripture records, 'Light and Darkness are principles, each in their own right and that their natures are completely distinct … The nature of Light is wisdom, that of Darkness is folly.'[87] Light and darkness, good and evil, soul and matter were the fundamental warring oppositions of the universe, and they informed the principal existential dilemmas of humanity.

In Islam, the metaphors of light and darkness are used in a similar way to these earlier traditions. For example, *An-Nûr*, or The Light, is one of the divine names of the *Qur'an* that contains repeated references to light and darkness as holy and unholy properties, respectively. In *The Cow*, we find, 'Allah is the Protecting Friend of those who believe. As for those who disbelieve, their patrons are false deities. They bring them out of the light into darkness.' (2:257) Allah is referred to as 'the Light of the heavens and the earth.' (29:96) And Mohammed, the Prophet, is described as a 'light from Allah.' (5:15)

Even a brief overview of the uses of the metaphors of light and darkness demonstrates how resilient and influential they have been. It is also evident that the metaphors have informed modern consciousness. Their integration has probably been so deep and successful that it is now perhaps impossible to dislodge them. Yet, we can gain much from attempting to do so. Even if the attempt is merely superficial, it might prove to be helpful because, sometimes, new insights appear when a metaphor is re-evaluated or recast in some way. Traditionally, such strategies are risky and evoke widespread resistance. As Joseph Campbell has pointed out, people can become 'stuck to their metaphors' and will defend them to the point of absurdity. He refers to the troubles in the Middle East as an example. Here the faithful of the three great religions of that region - Judaism, Christianity and Islam - cannot get on peacefully together because they subscribe to three different names for the same biblical God.[88]

Similarly, John Robinson ran into resistance, and voluminous criticism, in the 1960s when he suggested in his book *Honest to God* that it would be helpful to change our metaphor for thinking about God from something that is 'up there' and outside ourselves to something that is 'down here' and inside ourselves.[89] The proposal was all very well for mystics, Quakers and Jungians, but it was less so for literalists who still regard it as unacceptable. And yet, then as now, so many people have found his reorientation of the metaphor helpful. It enabled them to understand conventional religious teachings and benefit from them without having to subscribe to literal interpretations of religious phenomena. The same resistance, not to mention voluminous criticism, might lie in wait for the present thesis, but it is to that thesis that we must now turn. To begin with, let us consider light and darkness and their usefulness as metaphors.

The psalmist said, 'God is light.' The coincidence of these qualities has been expressed in one way or another throughout the centuries. Even in the twentieth century, Kenneth Clark, the Art Historian, wrote about artists' 'almost mystical rapture in the perception of light.'[90] But the association is not just spiritual nor purely aesthetic; it has natural references. Light is the principle of life. It makes things grow, and without it, life on earth would not be possible. After the winter solstice, when the light increases and the days lengthen, birds begin to lay their eggs. New life begins.

Light can also make things visible. It is the miraculous medium that bears the visible world to our senses. Sometimes in the process, the light that enables sight becomes the light that enables insight. Light can be quite justifiably called midwife to the birth of reason. Descartes saw the same connexion but reversed the order of symbols when he described the triumph of reason as 'the natural light of the mind.'[91] And it was the triumph of reason that characterised the Enlightenment - the period in early modern history in Europe and North America that ushered in modernity. The Enlightenment gave rise to the appearance of the natural and the social sciences. It introduced ideas of progress, individualism and individual human rights and eventually, it led to the establishment of democracy. From then onwards, it seemed that reason, and not just the vagaries of tradition, would guide what we would do, how we would do it, and what we would become.

However, the psalmist did not say, 'light is God.' That would be to secularise the very notion of God. It would reduce a profoundly mystical insight into that kind of simplistic physical perspective prevalent in some quarters of the modern world. In any case, whilst light can be reasonably described as the principle of life, so too can it be reasonably described as the principle of death. After all, excessive exposure to sunlight can cause malignant melanomas, squamous cell and basal cell carcinomas leading to illness and death in humans and animals. Light damages the DNA of cells, and it denatures and kills coral reefs. After the winter solstice, when the light increases and the days lengthen, the number of suicides begins to increase.[92]

And whilst it is evident that the Enlightenment had fostered genuine progress in human affairs, it is also evident that it could produce disaster. The science that gave us the possibility of sanitation, vaccination, anaesthetics, antibiotics and health-giving diets was also the science that gave us eugenics, industrial warfare and mad cow disease. Henry Ford, Benito Mussolini, J. Robert Oppenheimer, Josef Stalin and Bernard Madoff had more than enough Enlightenment fire run in their veins. Yet, their principal contributions to civilisation can hardly be described as progressive.

There are other paradoxes too. The light that can make things visible can also make things invisible. Where are the stars in daylight?

And whilst light has the power to illuminate, it also has the power to dazzle. The harsh clinical light of the halogen lamp can assist our efforts at the cutting edge of surgical techniques, but it can also sear, blind, disorientate and bleach the colours from our lives. It took the Romantics to point that out, and to suggest that there was far more to humanity than rational consciousness. John Keats described the damage that follows from the failure to recognise this. The relentless application of 'cold philosophy' to our perception of the world can 'clip an Angel's wings ... Empty the haunted air the gnomed mine ... Unweave a rainbow.'[93] Enlightenment philosophy was driven by the definitional imperative - the needless compulsion to 'conquer all mysteries by rule and line.' It was characterised by an over-cognitive, materialist tendency that was at once crudely superficial and chillingly convinced of its own progressive nature. That combination was to wreck countless lives.

Karl Marx, Friedrich Nietzsche and Sigmund Freud recognised the danger. Whilst each had their distinctive objections to the Enlightenment, they were at one when they argued that science could conceal as well as reveal. Science could divert our attention from the pursuit of wisdom and instead channel it towards the pursuit of technological ingenuity. They were also convinced that there were powerful forces at work in human affairs that were entirely unknown to us and which, in their various ways, enslaved us and made us wretched. Understanding these forces should be the main focus of our attention. After that, human emancipation, and not the getting of ever more material wealth, should be our principal concern. For Romantics and revolutionaries alike, the light of Enlightenment was not so revelatory after all. They felt conventional uses of the metaphor of light had been both simplistic and deeply deceptive.

But now, let us consider the metaphor of darkness. Just as it would be an error to see light as the sole principle of life and vision, so it would be equally an error to see darkness as the sole principle of death and blindness. Darkness has creative possibilities. It is in the darkness of the earth where the waters of life gather and are purified. It is in the darkness of soil where the seed germinates and finds the strength to push upwards into the light. It is in the darkness of the womb where the egg is fertilised and where the foetus grows into recognisable form. And it is in the darkness of another world where dreams arise. Dreams are the yearnings of the soul. They can become our inspiration and creativity. Theirs is the world of ancestry and myth and endless memory where nothing is forgotten. They inhabit that deep place of being, which knows what has been and has a clear sense of what is to come. Those who understand this will realise that dreams are the language of God.

And just as light can conceal, then so it is that darkness can make things visible. We can only see light when it is revealed by darkness. The sun is seen more distinctly at its eclipse. The scatter of winter stars is lost amongst the city lights but is at its most beautiful in the darkness of a forest. Lovers know that firelight pleases most in the dark.

Though there is always the paradox: we know that darkness can conceal; people and especially urban people, can become strangely confused and unnerved by the intensity of rural darkness. It is difficult to see in the dark. We can become disorientated, and that can make us afraid. Fear in the dark can sometimes lead to a fear of the dark. And the fear of darkness is a fear of life itself. Perhaps this is why we can speak of 'the dark night of the soul' when our very being is endangered. But then, the situation carries its own resolution because the dark night of the soul is necessary for salvation. In that darkness, we are closest to God. This is where insight arises, and wisdom is born. In the darkness of an oyster, the pearl is formed.

Our consideration of the metaphors of light and darkness suggest, therefore, that their common use in the modern world is both partial and confused. Far from light being preferable and darkness being non-preferable, it seems that *both* can lend themselves to an appreciation of creation and an understanding of the power of God. Light and darkness belong together. Each needs the other. They do not make sense without each other. The idea is not incongruous, nor is it new. In the third century CE Gnostic Gospel of Philip, we find:

Light and darkness, life and death, right and left, are inseparable twins. For the good are not wholly good nor the wicked wholly wicked, nor is life merely life, nor death merely death; each will return to its primal source. But those who transcend these apparent opposites are eternal ...[94]

Each being returned 'to its primal source' recalls the Taoist figure of the yin and yang, light and darkness reposing in contrasting and balanced states. Ways of looking at the natural complementarities of light and darkness have always been present in the history of thought. But the Taoist emphasis upon harmony, mutuality and non-preference provides us with an opportunity to create new uses and insights of the ancient metaphor for the present age.

To demonstrate the point, it is necessary to take our considerations a stage further. If we look at the symbol of the Tao once more, we can notice something else about it. As well as representing contrasting opposites in balanced harmony, it also suggests a certain *dynamic* relationship between light and darkness. As we look at it, it becomes clear that the image is invested with a kind of potential energy. Its very proportions indicate contrasts of permanence and change. It suggests waxing and waning, being and non-being, strength and weakness, overcoming and being overcome. Though the symbol of the Tao appears to be static, it is, in fact, a representation of that which is inherently dynamic. In the words of Claude Lévi-Strauss, it 'illustrates the reciprocal tempering of light and dark.'[95] This interaction is a powerful allegory of life itself.

The creative spirit has known this for centuries. We can find it throughout the arts. For example, in music, it appears in Beethoven's late string quartets. Here the tensions between Enlightenment Classicism and Romanticism vie with one another before finding a heightened resolution. In the visual arts, it emerges from the shadows of Michelangelo Merisi da Caravaggio and the Tenebrists. It culminates in Pre-Raphaelite aestheticism and the sublime work of John Atkinson Grimshaw. It can be found in writings of the Romantics and the Gothicists - and notably in the *chiaroscuro* of Bram Stoker's Gothic novel *Dracula*. *Dracula* was inspired by the setting of Grimshaw's work and translated his visual achievement into literature. Both Stoker and Grimshaw created and exemplified what Edmund Spenser called, 'A little glooming light, much like a shade,' in which a mood is evoked that can somehow summon and resonate with the deep evolving undulations of what it is to be alive.[96] As Paul Cézanne had it, 'Art is a harmony parallel to nature.'[97]

And we can go further and notice that wherever it is found - in music, in the visual arts or literature - it is that lilting of light and darkness that somehow holds opposition in unity and then miraculously *transcends* it to create something else. It creates an emergent property, a rare and beautiful state of being, that is imbued with nothing less than the divine principle. Nicholas of Cusa called it the *coincidentia oppositorum* - a form of consciousness that emerges from contrasting origins and leads to an exalted state of awareness.

The 'little glooming light' provides us with an insight into the deepest mysteries of life. Its contemplation can evoke a movement from physical to metaphysical realms. In psychological terms, it represents the appearance of a particular relationship between the light of consciousness and the darkness of unconsciousness.

The relationship is balanced, but its balance vacillates gently between one and the other. As such, it leads to a life that is neither shrouded in an unconsciously governed autism nor one that is lived perpetually in the full light of consciousness. In this shadowland, an altered state of consciousness is created where awareness is harmonic and transcendent. It is a mystical state that can provide us with salvation because it can invoke an experience of *being whole* - an experience that has been referred to as 'eternal life.'

What does all this mean in practical terms? To explore the idea further, it will help if we return to the symbol of the Tao. First of all, it is important to realise that symbols are not just abstract representations of things - they are potent products of the human psyche. They are potent in the sense that they can change our lives. This is because symbols participate in the nature of what they represent. If we contemplate the symbol of the Tao attentively, we will learn from it and through that process, our lives will be transformed.

The symbol of the Tao can teach us many things. Like all symbols, it has infinite meanings. But by way of illustration, we might begin by observing that the Tao suggests that there is never light without darkness and that there is never darkness without light. It indicates that life is far subtler than dualistic minds would have us believe. Every joyous moment carries with it the darker stuff of its undoing and every moment of sorrow carries with it the soft light of redemption. Joy and sorrow are inseparable, just as light and darkness are inseparable. One is not possible without the other.

The poet Kahlil Gibran expressed the idea when he wrote, 'The deeper that sorrow carves into your being, the more joy you can contain.'[98] We need the one to find a resolution in the other. How can we know how sweetly we have been dreaming until we have woken up? How can we understand the real meaning of safety until we have faced overwhelming danger? How can we appreciate health until we have felt the dull sap of illness? In a gentle way, the Tao can teach us that life is inherently paradoxical, and yet it is harmonic and somehow deeply beautiful.

The Tao might also teach us that it is the nature of things that the light of being will always give way to the darkness of non-being. And darkness always gives way to new light - to resurrection. In our busy lives, it is often necessary to remind ourselves of its inevitability. All things will pass, and when new circumstances emerge to take their place, these too will pass. The troubled mind might find comfort in this unalterable truth, and the untroubled mind might do well to heed it.

But how can this lead to an experience of eternal life? As with the previous examples we have considered in the world of art, a life lived in a harmony of opposites can produce two broad psychological effects. The first of these might be termed the integrative function. The integrative function is that which produces an *inclusive* state of awareness. It amounts to establishing a quantum psychology. It is the opposite of a light-orientated dualism. Instead of seeing life in terms of either/or, we begin to see it as *both*. The experience of being alive is understood as being at once awful and wonderful, beautiful and ugly, a pain and a pleasure. Once we realise that that is all there is and all we can have, we become tolerant of ambivalence and accepting of paradox. By not favouring light over darkness (and in the process acquiring an inclination towards making invidious distinctions, including the possibility of developing an unconscious racism) we can begin to acknowledge the creative primacy of light *and* darkness. We might then be able to accept our own darkness as well as the darkness of other people.

Consequently, we might develop a more temperate attitude to ourselves and others. When we 'judge not' between light and darkness, we are not ourselves judged. What follows is extraordinary. Anxiety and guilt are stilled. A distinctive calmness replaces inner turmoil. We move towards living in that spirit that takes away the occasion for all wars - wars within ourselves and wars with other people. A partial life that was lived anxiously in one half of an impossible duality is transformed into a whole life at peace with itself and then with creation.

If that is not miraculous enough, there is something else that occurs beyond most attempts to describe it. This is the second psychological effect, and it can be termed the transcendent function. The transcendent function produces what has been called in various traditions, enlightenment, samadhi, dignity, and states of grace, authenticity and mythic consciousness. It comes about when we can understand the significance of our own light and the light of other people. It ushers in a life lived in the consciousness of a transfigured world. In James Joyce's words, it is a life that has found a way to transmute 'the daily bread of experience into the radiant body of everliving life.'[99] It is a life that is illuminated by the softer lights and shadows of mystical perception. In this light, we can find the inner alchemy to reweave the rainbow and restore an Angel's wings. We can return to the innocence of a mythically starlit childhood world, but this time reconciled to the fathomless mystery of our lives and guided by the wisdom of redemption. In this fairest of lights, the light Walt Whitman called the 'rare and inexpressible light that illumines light itself,' we fulfil our purpose.[100] The fairest of lights is love - that which brings the re-union of the once separated. John O'Donohue wrote, 'Love is the light in which we see light. Love is the light in which we see each thing in its true origin, nature and destiny.'[101] And through the power of love, we enter into eternal life, where we incarnate the spirit of God. Here we see that light and darkness are one. Jeanne Guyon, the seventeenth-century French mystic, claimed as much when she wrote, 'To Him even darkness is light.'[102] And in this divine light, we can begin to participate in the mystery of who we are.

And who are we? Only God knows. But in dreams, it is given that we are children of eternity. She is where we came from, where all things belong, and where all things will return. Her powers of light and darkness raise us up and carry us gently in our days. When we live in her sway, we live eternally in time. That is what the soul yearns to do. For salvation is the garland of the soul. And in flowers of light, truth does flourish as the rose.

Flowers Of Light

What sayst thou, my fair flower-de-luce?

William Shakespeare Henry V, Act 5, Scene 2

In 1905, the English Pre-Raphaelite artist, Edward Robert Hughes [1851-1914] exhibited two watercolours. They are now titled *Day* and *Night*. Both are startlingly beautiful, but they have contrasting iconographies: *Day* [1895] is right facing and *Night* [1907] is left facing. They are extraverted and introverted in mood and represent the faces of light and darkness. *Day* portrays the head of a fair woman who is gazing ahead in anticipation. Her hair is adorned with a garland of pale flowers, like mayflowers, the flowers of spring. She is dayspring, the dawning of life into full

98

consciousness. Her companion, *Night* portrays the head of a dark woman whose gaze is downwards. She is not attending to the outer world, but instead, she seems to be reflecting upon the inner world of dreams. She is of shadows and the drawing down of life into the unconscious. By contrast, her garland is of stars - bright and diffuse in their loveliness, like flowers of light.

Night is a picture that seems to have a universal appeal, and consequently, it has been reproduced and sold as posters and greetings cards. This is hardly surprising. Its composition is sublime, elegant and somehow deeply powerful. Central to its success is the garland of stars. Its presence serves as a compositional trope, which effuses mystery. Hughes was an Aestheticist, who was devoted to an aesthetic principle rather than a moral one. Even so, the inclusion of the garland brings a distinctive spiritual air to the picture.

And what is more, that device has a traceable mythic history. For example, there can be little doubt that in creating *Night* Hughes had been influenced by his work two years earlier when he had helped the ageing William Holman Hunt to complete *The Lady of Shalott* [1905]. The influence is clear: the model is similar, as is her dark countenance and the scintillations in her hair. During the same period, Hughes had also assisted Hunt with the St Paul's Cathedral version of *The Light of the World*. It was probably from the intense first-hand experience of working on this picture that his understanding of the power of dramatic illumination was heightened and later conveyed to the radiant stars that grace

8. Hunt, *The Lady of Shalott*

9. Rossetti, *The Blessed Damozel*

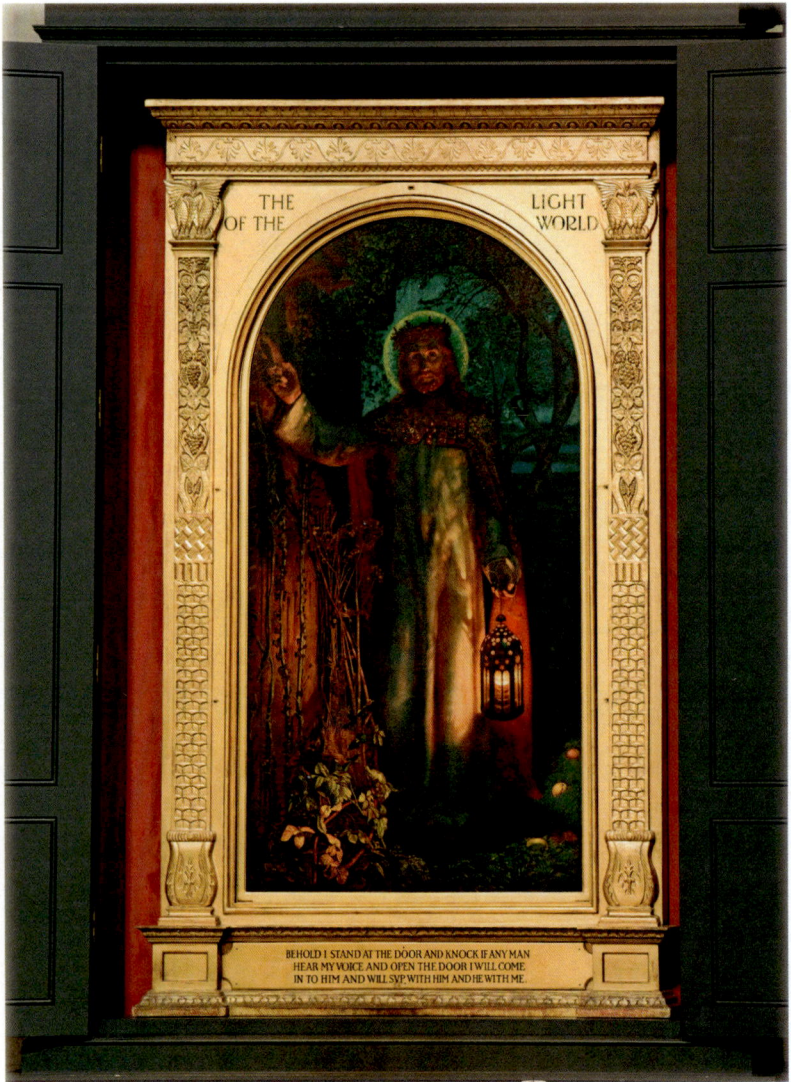

10. Hunt, *The Light of the World*

Night's hair. Hughes must also have been familiar with the work of Dante Gabriel Rossetti. In particular, he must have known about *The Blessed Damozel* as a picture [1874] and as a poem [1850] 'and the stars in her hair were seven.'[103] In this, Rossetti was following a tradition as old as history itself. Throughout the Middle Ages, pictures and sculptures of the Virgin Mary were often crowned with stars.[104] Even earlier, the Babylonian goddess, Ishtar, the Queen of Night and arguably, the archetype of the Virgin Mary[105] and whose name meant 'star' was often represented as being crowned with stars. The same is true of the powerful Egyptian goddess Isis, 'the Queen of the Stars,' who was for centuries associated with Sirius, the bright star at the foot of the constellation, Orion. In the *Book of Revelation*, we read of Michael and his angels battling with a dragon in defence of the 'woman clothed with the sun, and the moon under her feet, and upon her head a crown of twelve stars' and who was 'travailing in birth.' Janet and Stewart Farrar suggest that this is an allusion to Isis and the birth of her son, Horus, god of the sun, and the battles she and others had had with Seth, god of darkness.[106] So that, in creating *Night,* it is probable that Hughes had evoked one of the earliest known goddesses in Ishtar, and perhaps the most influential of goddesses in Isis, and he had done so with flowers of light.

And there are flowers of light. Shakespeare called them fleurs-de-luce, an English variant of the French, fleurs-de-lis, which means 'lily flower' or iris. The iris is associated heraldically with the Virgin Mary, and with the kings of France. This is because tradition has it that the Virgin had presented Clovis I, the King of France, with an iris to signify that his kingship was assured, not by Papal decree or any secular authority, but directly by the will of God.

There are many examples of an association of the iris with the Virgin Mary in sacred art. Typically an iris appears somewhere in the picture, or the Virgin carries an iris or she wears a crown of irises or fleurs-de-lis on her head.[107] This association is inherited from earlier traditions. Peter Bersuire, the fourteenth-century French monk, suggests in his *Reportorium Morale* that the iris was a symbol of divinity and was associated with the rainbow. He gives as his authority the *Book of Revelation*, where an angel appears crowned with a rainbow and carrying a book of prophecies intended for John the Divine. Bersuire might have referred instead to the flood and God's rainbow covenant in *Genesis* as his source of inspiration. It is, after all, probably more widely known, but then there is a significant difference between the two. In *Genesis*, the rainbow is described as a 'token' of God's covenant. In *Revelation*, the rainbow is associated with a divine intercessor who was a messenger. It is entirely possible that this later allusion was preferable to Bersuire because he may have associated it with an older and more elemental tradition.

Indeed, the connection between the iris and the rainbow predates *Revelation* by several centuries. According to the first century CE Greek herbalist Pedanius Dioscorides in his seminal *De Materia Medica*, the iris plant was named after Iris, the Greek goddess of the rainbow. Presumably, this came about through an association with the rainbow because of its iridescent colours and the bow-shaped striations of the flower. In Greek mythology, it was Iris who carried souls to their final resting place in the Elysian Fields. Like Bersuire's *Revelation* angel, she was a divine intercessor and messenger of the Gods. She travelled from heaven to earth with a winged staff to declare the will of the Gods to those on earth. As she moved through the sky, the trail of her coloured robe produced the rainbow. Henry Wadsworth Longfellow describes her wonderfully in his poem: 'Flower–de-Luce':

> *Thou art the iris, fair among the fairest,*
> *Who, armed with golden rod,*
> *And winged with celestial azure, bearest*
> *The message of some god.*

Iris was handmaiden to Hera, the sister and wife of Zeus. Hera means 'Lady', and in Greek mythology, she was 'Queen of Heaven.' Both Iris and Hera were to influence later descriptions of the Virgin Mary. The Virgin inherited an association with Iris because she too was the divine intercessor between God and the world. She inherited an association with Hera because she too was addressed as 'Our Lady, Queen of Heaven.' In the eighth century BCE, Hesiod referred to Iris, goddess of the rainbow, in the *Homeric Hymns*. She was also mentioned in Homer's *Iliad*, which was written in the ninth century BCE. In turn, Homer's inspiration was even older than this - indeed his source is to be found in one of the earliest known works of literature, *The Epic of*

Gilgamesh. The *Epic* was discovered and translated by George Smith, the English Assyriologist, in 1872. He was working in the British Museum with artefacts collected by Henry Creswicke Rawlinson during his archaeological excavations in Nineveh, in what we would now call, Iraq. There were twelve cuneiform tablets in all, and these have been dated to around 2000 BCE. Other versions of the *Epic* have now come to light, and these represent various re-workings of the texts by several Mesopotamian cultures. In Tablet XI of one of these versions, there is an account of a great flood. This tells of Ishtar, who following the destruction of the earth by the deluge, takes off the necklace of lapis lazuli encircling her neck and sets it in the sky as a rainbow to prevent such an event ever happening again.

The term 'flower of light' is therefore, an appropriate one for the iris. Its affinities with the rainbow, the Queen of Heaven, ancient covenants and intercessory links between heaven and earth mark it out as a symbol of divinity. Yet there is something else that can be learned from it. Often it is clear what symbols represent and how they came to represent what they do. However, it is not always apparent why a symbol has been chosen and in which sense it is appropriate.

Nevertheless, it is possible to explore the meaning of a symbol even when there is no historical evidence or obvious linguistic or other indicative associations to help us. One way of doing this is simply to look at the symbol. If symbols are observed and considered imaginatively, it is sometimes possible to understand the perceptions of those who have gone before us and who bore the symbol in the first place. We can use our subjectivity to understand theirs. So let us apply the technique of what might be termed, 'restorative symbolism' to see if we can gain some understanding of the symbology of the iris.

But before we do, it is important to consider a possible objection to this proposal and the reasoning behind it so that our application of the technique can be recognised as being legitimate. A rational critic might say, 'Surely, pre-modern people would have no time to pontificate upon the possible significance of the number of petals on a flower? Their days would have been taken up with practical matters - securing a livelihood and feeding families.' But whilst this objection might seem to be reasonable, it would be wrong. Indeed, it would be an example of what ethnographers call the 'fallacy of tempocentrism.' It would make the mistake of assuming that modern ways of thinking were prevalent amongst pre-modern peoples. Even though we share a common humanity with those who lived before us, we should never expect that they made sense of the world in the same way as we do. Ever since Edward Burnett Tylor's monumental publication *Primitive Culture*, it has been acknowledged that earlier generations perceived the world animistically.[108] They classified and understood things according to perceived similarities rather than in terms of what we would regard as objective criteria. For them, nothing was accidental. Appearances always meant something. It was an indication of the purpose and the otherworldly significance of things.[109]

In Europe, the connexion between appearance and purpose had undoubtedly been established in Classical times. Pedanius Dioscorides and Galen of Pergamum, the Roman physician, had formulated it in the first century CE. By the medieval period, the idea that the appearance of a plant was a sign of its significance was commonplace throughout much of the world. In the twelfth century, Hildegard of Bingen had developed the idea through her concept of 'Veriditas' or 'greenness' as the divine principle that penetrates every aspect of life. In the sixteenth century, Phillip von Hohenheim, the Swiss botanist, otherwise known as Paracelsus, did much to disseminate the tradition, as did Jakob Böhme, of Görlitz in Germany in the seventeenth century. Böhme developed the concept of the 'doctrine of signatures' in his book, *De Signatura Rerum* or *The Signature of all Things*. He consolidated the earlier classical ideas and suggested that careful observation of a plant - the shape of its leaves and flowers, its colours and its place of growth could reveal its divine purpose. Böhme's ideas proved to be a significant influence in the development of western herbalism, but they also found sympathy amongst philosophers, theologians, the Romantic poets and artists, including the Pre-Raphaelites and the Aestheticists, and even in Hughes himself.

Carl Gustav Jung felt that he was able to account for this. According to him, the very notion of the doctrine of signatures is based upon an unconscious logic that is universally distributed throughout humanity and which, therefore, carries a universal intuitive appeal.[110] Therefore, a spontaneous perception of there being a link between resemblance and identity, and between what something looks like and its symbolic significance had a powerful and enduring influence on how people thought and continue to think about the world.

So what can we make of it - the garden iris - this flower of light that blooms in May, the month that was once so widely associated with the Virgin Mary and Virgin goddesses the world over?[111] What can we make of its leaves, or 'Mary's Swords of Sorrow,' or the appearance of its early flower that D. H. Lawrence called its 'fine proud spike of purple?'[112] Certainly, they are perfect foils for one another and together, they create an aesthetic fusion that is at once sculptural, and a triumph of beauty.

11. Bearded Iris - *Iris germanica*

When in full flower, the iris attains a graceful three-dimensional form, which defines majesty. Its elegance is arranged in threes. There are three azure 'falls' that have deep marbled throats of purple and white. Each one has a delicate 'beard' that leads to the very heart of the bloom, where three stamens, the organs of conception, are located. Rising above the falls are the 'standards' or 'flags' - erect petals of purple and blue. The full flower provided the natural archetype of the heraldic fleurs-de-lis. And for the French Crusaders who first bore them, the three petals of the fleurs-de-lis signified the virtues of faith, wisdom and valour.

The masculine and feminine characteristics of the iris are expressed in a trimerous symmetry. The iris embodies threeness. It speaks to us in threes. So what might this have signified to earlier generations? A comprehensive analysis of the significance of the number three is not appropriate here, but several indicative observations can be made, and these might assist the process of symbolic restoration.

A brief survey of cultures across the world is enough to show that the number three has and is regarded as an auspicious number.[113] In religion, we find the highest order of beings, objects, events and meanings are expressed in threes. In Christianity, the essential and divine nature of God is described as Father, Son and Holy Spirit. In the Wiccan tradition, we find the illuminating notion of the 'Triple Goddess,' Virgin, Mother and Crone. In ancient Egypt, there is Osiris, Isis and Horus. The Babylonians had Sin, Shamash and Ishtar. In Hinduism, there is the *Trimurti*, or the triple Godhead of Brahma, Vishnu and Shiva. In the Nordic tradition, there is the divine triad of Odin, Thor and Freya. Arguably, all these are informed by the same archetypal event that has attended the experiences of people throughout the world since consciousness emerged - the three dark days of the moon which occur every month, before it miraculously resurrects as a new moon - an event to marvel at and invest with hope. Jung thought that the number three has a deeper, mystical significance. For him, three is the number of transcendence. One is original unity; two represents duality, the emergence of pairs of opposites and three represents that which goes beyond duality and combines duality with non-duality. That is to say, by combining two with one, the number three achieves transcendence.[114] Aristotle wrote, 'Of two things, or men, we say 'both', but not 'all': three is the first number to which the term 'all' has been appropriated.'[115]   'For as the Pythagoreans say, the world and all that is in it is determined by the number three, since beginning, middle and end give the number of an 'all', and the number they give is the triad. And so having taken these things from nature as (so to speak) laws of it, we make further use of the number three in the worship of the Gods.'[116] Jung agreed with this. He thought the number three was an archetype of the unconscious, or a predisposition to perceive something in a particular way. Archetypes occur universally, and therefore the images that represent them are generally seen to be of special significance.

If we accept Jung's interpretation, we can see that the iris must have had a numinous significance to those earlier generations who were familiar with it. According to the Kabbalistic tradition, the number three represents stability and balance. But this ascription can be developed in the case of the iris. Its leaves and flowers combine to produce a wondrous profusion of masculine and feminine qualities with a trimerous composition that resonates with the very nature of androgynous divinities and therefore, ultimately, the iris can be seen as embodying *divine* transcendence.

However, our restorative symbolism should not end there. The morphology of the iris is not simply trimerous. Its three standards, three falls and three stamens represent three times three. It embodies three times the power of three and by so doing presents itself to the world as a quite extraordinary object. It is a representation of the pre-eminent number nine.

Joseph Campbell has suggested nine relates to the 'Goddess of Many Names' (whose names include: Devī, Inanna, Ishtar, Isis, Astarte, Artemis and Aphrodite) and he associates the Virgin Mary as a later manifestation in this tradition.[117] In numerological terms, nine is a magical number. In *Macbeth*, we find the three witches casting a spell, 'Thrice to thine and thrice to mine, and three again to make up nine.'[118] One of the reasons the number nine is considered to be magical is because it is the number of empirical immortality. When it dies, it is born again. When multiplied by another number, it disappears: $2 \times 9 = 18$. But then it appears again: $1 + 8 = 9$, and $3 \times 9 = 27$ and $2+7 = 9$ and so on, throughout the multiplication series. The Catholic Church recognised this quality and proposed that since the number ten is the *numerus maximus* - the number that represents perfection because it is the completeness of two hands and contains all the other numbers - the number nine is less than perfect, but it always contains the possibility of resurrection. In terms of Catholic theology, the number nine represents humanity's imperfection and its seeking of heavenly grace through prayer and by the intercession of Our Lady and the saints. Hence, the *Kyrie*, a petition and response, is said nine times in every mass. *Novenas* are nine days of devotion and at three times each day nine bells mark the *Angelus*, devotional prayers said morning, noon and night to commemorate the Annunciation or the announcement of the angel Gabriel to Mary that she would bear the child of God. The term 'Angelus' means literally 'Angel Messenger.' The *Angelus* is said in the Roman Catholic, Anglo-Catholic and some Lutheran Churches. Its fundamental purpose is to celebrate the Incarnation, or the descent of the divine into human life. It marks the miracle of the birth of Christ within the imagination. In other words, nine, the number of beginnings and endings, represents the hope of new life.

The association of the iris with eternal life is also invoked by a further consideration. Look at what is perhaps its most startling aspect - the colour of its flowers. The deeply iridescent blue of its petals is powerful and redolent with associations of the Virgin Mary.[119] Ever since the Spanish painter, Francisco Pacheco, gave the instruction in his book *The Art of Painting* in 1649, blue has been the traditional colour of Mary's celestial cloak. But in a more immediate sense, blue is the colour of a clear sky. The blue of the sky has been drawn down into the flower. A part of the sky, where, traditionally, heaven is located, has entered the world. It is 'heavenly blue' and symbolically it represents eternity in the midst of time.

Finally, in this restorative symbolism, let us consider where the iris grows. Originally, it was said to have flourished in the Garden of

Eden. But now, in its various forms, the iris grows right across the Northern Hemisphere. Like people, it can survive well in a range of conditions, but like people too, it grows to its full stature and beauty when it is well fed and nourished by the light. The Romans introduced *Iris germanica*, to Britain, where it is well established as a common garden plant. But here, all too often, its full beauty and majesty go unacknowledged and it is largely left to take care of itself. There are some notable exceptions, however. Irises are sometimes found in British churchyards. Those of Tilbury-juxta-Clare in Essex and of Drayton Beauchamp in Buckinghamshire are prime examples. Richard Mabey claims irises have become naturalized in these places as a result of their bright orange seed capsules being used in winter grave bouquets and then subsequently germinating.[120] This may well be true, but there is reason to believe another factor might have been at work. A survey of the Mediterranean countries, the Middle East and other regions that were influenced by the Greek and later, the Roman Empires, indicates 'mourning irises' *(Iris susiana)* are still planted on graves, in churchyards and other sacred places. Iris flowers last for only a few days, and the rest of the year, it is fair to say the plant is unprepossessing. It is entirely possible, therefore, that in Britain as elsewhere, irises have been planted for symbolic and not for decorative reasons. This tender gesture of mourning evokes a folk-memory. It recalls the Goddess and the miracle of being borne gently to a new life in the Elysian Fields.

But if folk memories of the iris have survived, they are not substantial. We have forgotten more than we have remembered. But just as the iris was thought to raise us up to new life, so perhaps the time has come when we might raise the iris up to new life, or at least to a life of renewed significance. A symbol can be revivified if it is liberated from it from its previous context and considered in the present. When this is done, many of the earlier meanings will remain, but sometimes, new connotations will emerge along with new associations of earlier ones. In that process, these meanings are restored to modern consciousness, and the final stage of our restorative symbolism will have been achieved.

What might a renewed significance of the iris be? Perhaps we could liken it to the 'blue flower' of the Romantics - that emblem given to us by Georg Friedrich Freiherr von Hardenberg, who called himself Novalis, and whose longing to go beyond the immediate givens in life and find a metaphysical home has struck a chord with writers, artists, philosophers and theologians ever since. His desire met theirs. The blue flower was an expression of a primal yearning, a yearning to escape the suffering imposed by the dualities of time and return to eternity. This desire calls to mind the rainbow motif of transcendence to some numinous place. So the blue flower could be seen as representing a longing to return to Paradise, or to its biographical equivalent, the primordial bliss of being held in our mother's arms. It is a longing close to every generation, and for that reason, the iris, this flower of Novalis, might serve as a symbol of eternal life.

In *Day* and *Night*, Edward Robert Hughes has created images that are opposites and which define each other. They are like the warp and weft of our experience, the faces of Logos and Eros, whose expressions speak to us of temporal and eternal life.

In *Night* we have a picture that is evocative of eternal life. It is an icon of how our lives might be lived. For eternal life is not one marshalled and marched perpetually to the tick and tock of time. Rather, it is a life graced and guided by the celestial light of stars. In eternal life, we are crowned by light - a light 'crowning the aspirations of thought, illuminating the paths of imagination, spreading the radiance of vision.'[121] In its presence, we feel the joy of being alive. By its strength, our souls are carried gently to the rainbow. And through its power; we awake to see the face of God.

Time And Eternity

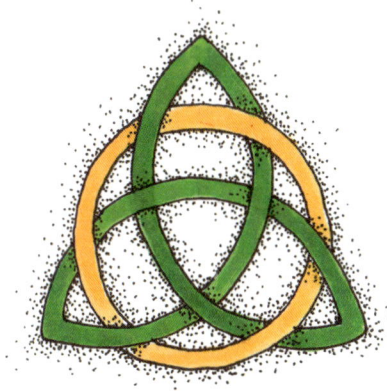

12. Sayers, Celtic symbol of time and eternity

Meister Eckhart, the fourteenth-century Thuringian theologian, metaphysician and mystic, has given the modern world a compelling model of the relationship between time and eternity. His model can be used to provide an account of how the past and the future can be assimilated to the present in such a way that reunion and prophecy become explicable.

The model also provides the possibility of interpreting the relationship between time and eternity in terms of the dialectics between unconsciousness and consciousness. It can also account for the subsequent emergence of those altered states of consciousness that can be collectively described as experiences of eternal life. So that, the model can be used to suggest an ontological link between the unconscious and eternity and its expression as myth, as well as between consciousness and time and its expression as history. Seen in this way, the 'eternal moment' becomes characterised as a transient state of awareness that is informed by both unconscious and conscious elements and which offers its subjects miraculous opportunities.

In the writings of Meister Eckhart, we find a constructive model of the relationship between time and eternity. It is presented as an image of God, who is located in eternity. He is gazing at the historical drama that is the world in all its diversity. From this eternal vantage point, God can see everything that was, everything that is, and everything that will be, and he can do all this simultaneously. Eckhart writes:

For the *now* wherein God made the first man, and the *now* wherein the last man disappears, and the *now* I speak in, all are the same in God where there is but *the now*.[122]

And elsewhere:

… in eternity is no before or after; the happenings of the past millennium and the future one and now, in eternity are all the same. God's doings of a thousand years ago and now and a thousand years to come are but one single act. It follows that the man who is exalted above time into eternity will do with God what he did in the past and also what he does in the next thousand years.[123]

This imagery provides us with an opportunity to take Eckhart's metaphor further and by so doing, create new meanings and thereby differentiate our understanding of the notions of time and eternity. In particular, the model helps us to understand that from the perspective of eternity, the past, the present and the future are one. That is to say, they can be conceptualised as being genuinely concurrent. What heuristic value might this model offer? One possibility is that the past and the future are potentially experientially contiguous with the present. Put simply, this means that from the standpoint of eternity, the past and the future can be brought into the present. The objects and events of the past, and the future can be experienced in the present. Indeed, the model might provide us with a way of accounting for a sense of the past being folded into the present. Laurent Olivier has described the past as 'lying in wait in the folds of present time, forgotten but in reality ready to leap out like a cat.'[124] We might go further and suggest that Eckhart's model and Olivier's notion of the folding of time provides us with a way of accounting for a sense of the future being folded into the present. This might help us to understand how prophecy arises.

These are weighty ideas, and we can take them further. But before we can do so, we have to ask the question, 'what are time and eternity?' If our analysis is to be useful, we have to move from a fourteenth-century metaphor towards a set of twenty-first-century metaphysical propositions which we can explore. Philosophers throughout the ages have attempted definitions of these terms, and the best they have achieved are working definitions in the service of particular lines of thought. We can do no better here, but we can offer a distillation of Eckhart's ideas. Of the two concepts, time is the easier to define. Its definition can be provided in simple prose: time is that which is attributed to the articulating principle of a series of events. The definition of eternity is harder to achieve, and consequently, this is usually expressed poetically or metaphorically. A typical definition is, eternity is that which is above, below, beyond or outside of time.

Following the work of Augustine, Boethius and Anselm, the distinction between time and eternity has been made implicitly and explicitly. In many cases, it has been central to theorists' work. These notions have been elaborated to the point where there are now widely-used conventional contemporary definitions. However, one aspect of this work has been comparatively neglected. This involves questions about the ontological status of time and eternity. Are these subjective or objective qualities? In modified Kantian terms, should they be understood as phenomena or as a dimension of the thing-in-itself? There are, of course, intriguing possibilities in considering them as *both*. It is outside the scope of the present analysis to address this matter comprehensively, but the grounds for our analysis must be made clear before we proceed. The position adopted here is admittedly simplistic, and it rests upon the observation that whilst the concepts of time and eternity are undeniably categories of experience, little else can be safely assumed about them. Therefore, for our purposes, the terms 'time' and 'eternity' will be regarded as subjective qualities, and by extension, they will be regarded as *psychological* phenomena.

Although this position is partial, it is also useful in that it allows us to bring the discourse into the realms of the familiar. It also enables us to make further analytic progress. For example, the question might be asked, if time and eternity are assumed to be psychological phenomena, what would be the best way of studying them? Since these are qualities that cannot be defined adequately enough to enable us to identify, measure and manipulate them in controlled experimental settings, it is arguable that an experimental approach to their study would be inappropriate.[125]

However, a hermeneutic approach, such as psychoanalysis which employs conceptual analysis, would be ideal. When psychoanalysis is applied, the results are both immediate and compelling. For example, assertions that time is linear and sequential correspond to psychoanalytic claims that this is also the case with conscious thought.[126] And assertions that eternity is non-linear and non-sequential[127] correspond to psychoanalytic claims that this is also the case with the unconscious.[128] Other correlations can be made between time and consciousness, and between eternity and the unconscious. For example, there is a correspondence between time and the progressive dualism of consciousness and between eternity and the non-progressive, non-dualism of unconsciousness.[129] The unconscious is typically described as 'archaic,' 'primordial,' 'pre-logical,' or 'pre-linguistic' and hence, not given to the development of sequential logic.[130] There is sufficient congruence here to be indicative.

We are now in a position to produce more comprehensive definitions of time and eternity in the light of those explicit and implicit connections outlined above. These working definitions will also serve as conceptual hypotheses for the analysis that follows.

121

Psychologically speaking, an awareness of time is a function of consciousness and ultimately, of thought. Consequently, time is commonly experienced as linear and sequential.[131] It is predominantly an experience of becoming. The dynamic of time is progress, and the nature of its discourse is historical. Its expression is rational, and its apprehension is through the exercise of reason. The effects of this are manifold. Isaac Newton's formulation of ideas about classical mechanics provided the concept of 'absolute time,' or time that passes uniformly and independently of the world. These Enlightenment ideas were gradually generalised, so that the modern world adopted a particular view of time. Not only was this evident in common sense perceptions of the world, but also it became the standard in science and technology trade and commerce, transport, government, law and administration.

In psychological terms, the experience of eternity is a function of the unconscious, and like the unconscious, it is often described as being timeless or above, below, beyond or outside of time. It is predominantly the experience of being. The dynamic of eternity is archaic, and the nature of its discourse is mythical. Its mode of expression is non-rational, and its apprehension is intuitive. A preponderant experience of eternity was the basis of pre-modern life. And, if the apparent growth of new forms of religiosity in the Western world is indicative, then increasingly, it is becoming the basis of post-modern life.[132]

There are numerous psychological references to the effects

of the integration of unconscious elements within the realms of consciousness.[133] In general, these refer to the mediating potential of symbols embedded in myth, religion, art, politics and elsewhere. The proposal is that symbols are characterised by their referential affinity to both unconsciousness and consciousness. In other words, since symbols and symbolic narratives have bivalency for both aspects of psychological life, it is postulated that they can serve to fuse the one with the other. When this happens to a significant degree through the influence of religious or other forms of symbolic representation, altered states of consciousness will occur. These altered states have been variously described as states of grace, dignity, samadhi, nirvana, participation mystique, authenticity and self-actualization and are best described as numinous or peak experiences.

Even a temporary integration of unconsciousness with consciousness can be seen as an integration of the eternal with the temporal. An event of this kind might be termed an 'eternal moment' and recurrent states of integration might be termed 'eternal life.' (A definition of eternal life that stresses concurrency is no doubt partial, but it is nevertheless practical. The nature of eternal life has been considered both in terms of everlasting life and as an elevated state of soul experienced in the present. There are Biblical and other authorities to support each notion.[134] The position taken here will avoid commenting upon the relative merits of these, and from the outset, it will assume a Johannine-derived perspective on eternal life as a lived experience.)

Joseph Campbell wrote, '… the experience of eternity right here and now, in all things, whether thought of as good or as evil, is the function of life.'[135] This courageous claim contains an entire cosmology. Within it lies the implication that eternal life is a temporal state of varying duration in which selflessness and a sense of harmony with everything in the created world underpins a realisation that the apparent truths, dramas, complexities and frustrations of the temporal world are empirically superficial and probably, deceptive. This stands in direct contrast to an experience of life lived purely in what Walter Benjamin called 'homogenous and empty time,'[136] from which a rootless condition arises, where pleasure-seeking accompanies an otherwise deadened and joyless existence. According to Campbell eternal life brings with it a sense of union with the source of life itself [137] as well as a sense of what Richard Gregg calls 'unitive knowledge' or an intuitive understanding, that the past and the future are contained within the eternal moment.[138]

Robert Ornstein describes how mystical traditions throughout the world deliberately cultivate altered perceptions of time.[139] Typically this alteration is achieved through dream or trance states, or through ritual, prayer, meditation, dance, drama, fasting, recitation of, or concentration upon, a narrative or through the use of psychotropic substances. Indeed, an alteration can be achieved by any activity that Mircea Eliade suggests has the effect of arresting 'profane temporal duration.'[140]

In these altered states, Paul Tillich suggests that, 'the spirit is fulfilled by eternity.'[141] It was William Blake who saw 'the Past, Present & Future existing all at once Before me.'[142] When this happens, the mystic is as close as it is possible to be in experiencing Eckhart's notion of the position of God from his vantage point outside of time. The brilliant Quaker writer, Lorna Marsden wrote, 'At this frontier - a frontier before which a man stands totally naked - sight returns. On the far horizon a light is reflected from both past and future, and it is a single light.'[143] Familiar objects and events of the past are experienced in detail as a numinous presence. One's childhood, the sounds and impressions of school and neighbourhood, along with a sense of the bodily presence of loved ones appear to be close. On the other hand, objects and events of the future are not familiar because they have never been experienced in time. Their appearance in the present is, therefore, qualitatively different. It is a sense of foreknowledge. Future objects and events are felt distinctly but they are perceived as numinous presences which are vague. Marsden makes the point eloquently:

In the mists ahead of us move already shapes that we dimly recognise. It is in our affirmations of these clouded shapes that they will take form as truth. (In the same way the hypotheses of creative science take form.)[144]

In such circumstances, the sensing of the past and future are Jean-Pierre de Caussade's 'sacraments of the present moment.'[145] We might even speculate that in the sacraments of the present moment arising out of dreams, these 'dimly recognised' phenomena can be affected by the mechanisms of dreamwork.[146] In particular, the processes of condensation and displacement might operate so that shifts of the *personae dramatis* will sometimes occur. The young man in Manchester, who dreamt in 1971 that he was standing on Platform 9 in York station waiting nervously for the train to take him to university to begin an undergraduate course in marine biology might have had precognition of his daughter who, thirty-six years later, in 2007, was standing on Platform 9 in York station waiting nervously for the train to take her to university to begin an undergraduate course in marine biology.[147] The young man's dream was salutary. To paraphrase D. H. Lawrence, 'This, if he knew it, was his life and his eternity.'

All the world's major religions have their mystics - those who have become suffused with spirituality. In terms suggested by this essay, these people might be described as those whose strength of faith to their religious practices has resulted in their attaining more or less permanent states of eternal life. Through faith, some people have become beautifully orientated between the way they perceive the past and the way they perceive the future, their myths and their prophecies. Consequently, they can live their lives as securely as a traveller confident of their position between the Global Positioning System coordinates that define the progress of a journey. They are the poets and prophets. Theirs is to see clearly and, as John Ruskin wrote, 'To see clearly is poetry, prophecy and religion - all in one.'[148]

Eckhart worked with a metaphor to model the relationship between two of the greatest mysteries that can come before us - time and eternity - and we must do the same. Of course, what is offered here, by way of an exploration of Eckhart's model, is not based in any way upon empirical analysis. Instead, it is a way of thinking about aspects of our lives that must forever remain in the realms of the mysterious - that which cannot be truly comprehended. But it does seek to be illuminative, and it does so on the grounds of its 'intrinsic reasonableness.' More than this, it constitutes a myth, or more accurately, a mythopoeic narrative, through which we might begin to reflect upon the wonder of our lives.

Epilogue

We have come to the end of the book, and the question arises, 'what *is* the truth about time and eternity and their workings in our everyday lives?' The answer I must give will probably look like a pointless riddle. Having written with conviction my thoughts about time and eternity, I would have to admit that I do not know what *the* truth about them is. You see, it is my conviction that there is no truth other than the ones we adopt or create for ourselves. In the end, all I have is *my own* truth, and I have done my best to present it to you here as honestly and as faithfully as I can. Sociologists call this 'relational truth.' It is the truth, as seen from a particular perspective. What I have given here is a truth as seen from my perspective.

Friedrich Nietzsche thought that what we call the truth is merely our familiarity with the 'customary metaphors' of social convention. For him, the very idea of 'truth' is a metaphor. In his essay, 'On Truth and Lying in a Non-Moral Sense' he wrote, 'What, then, is truth? A moveable army of metaphors, metonymies, anthropomorphisms.' Nietzsche believed we could only think in parables. What we call truth is our faltering attempts to make sense of things, but these can never be the truth about the way things really are.

I think Nietzsche had a point. Not that there is anything intrinsically wrong with our using metaphors; they are all we have to make sense of the world. Ultimately what matters is not whether something is true or false, but how *useful* it is to us, how it can serve as a guide to

128

living a good life and dying a good death. In this respect, perhaps we should seek out those truths we can practise most comfortably.

At the same time, we might remind ourselves that our truths might be what we feel as right to live by and right to die by, but they should never stand in the way of our compassion. People should not find themselves in conflict with others simply because they each subscribe to different sets of extended metaphors. And, over the centuries, this is what has happened. People have a long history of killing for metaphors.

I have done all I can, and now, it is my dearest wish that you think about what I have written and see if it has anything to say to you. I hope it will. May *All is One Love* bring a measure of light into your lives.

The Dream

He fell asleep by a lakeside in Cumbria - a place of gentle reflections, where dreams are dreamed and the souls of the dead meet and marry the souls of the living.

Not for him the pounding heart over volcanic rock and mountain springs. Not for him, the view from high peaks reached by power and sweat and burning lungs. He was dragged down by tiredness and caught in the embrace of autumnal light. Lapping waters called him from their depths, and he was carried to the lilting space between worlds, a space where ancient poets whispered in shadows, and fire and frost cleaved deep into his helplessness. And there, the past was recalled, and its grace filled the present and revealed a vision of the future.

129

Before him were his people, the people of his flesh and sacrifice. They met in their twos and threes, not seeing him, not knowing him, and yet talking about him as though he were their own. These were the authors of his life, the ones risen in the blood and borne in time: familiar faces which were somehow beyond his telling. And it was enough, enough to awaken him into that fullness of life which is beyond all yearning.

And when they came down from the mountainside, it was enough to tell them that a dream had held him and now, all is one love.

Appendix

A. Transpersonal Psychology

Transpersonal psychology is a fruit of the Enlightenment, but then, it's reasonable to argue that all modern perspectives in psychology are fruits of the Enlightenment. However, transpersonal psychology is a particularly remarkable progeny. It was formed from surprisingly diverse and sometimes conflicting origins, including elements of both Enlightenment and anti-Enlightenment thinking. This essay will trace aspects of the development of transpersonal psychology to reveal something of its nature and purpose.

The Enlightenment

The Enlightenment was a social movement that swept through Europe and North America in the seventeenth, eighteenth and nineteenth centuries and ushered in modernity. It's known as the Age of Reason because it took as its guiding star the idea that *reason* should be the only legitimate guiding principle for all intellectual and social activities. Several generations of intellectual elites thought this was how genuine progress could be achieved. Humanity would free itself from centuries of ignorance and build a future based upon the application of reason. Reason would determine what people would do, how they would do it and what the social world would become.

The Enlightenment changed the world. It fuelled the Industrial Revolution and enabled significant developments not only in philosophy but also in agriculture, economics, mathematics, engineering, science and technology, transport, industrial production, medicine and law. The success of these developments gave rise to new *mechanistic* ways of understanding the natural and social worlds.

It saw the emergence of the social sciences. Ideas about progress, individualism, liberty, equality and democracy began to appear and take root. In various parts of the world, the calendar, currency, units of measurement and city street patterns were replaced by rationally-determined alternatives. Political revolutions brought nation-states into being. The old ways of production and trade were overturned, and capitalism emerged. Populations began to increase exponentially.

Reactions to the Enlightenment

Inevitably, these developments weren't universally welcomed. Resistance movements appeared. These were often characterised by a rejection of what might be termed Enlightenment absolutism. They couldn't accept its tendency to deify reason and exclude all other ways of thinking about life and enjoying it. They yearned to return to what were perhaps naive notions of earlier and more wholesome ways of doing things. There was a growing interest in collecting and preserving local history, genealogies, customs and traditions, archives, manuscripts, folk tales, song, music and dance. Gentlemen archaeologists led the quest to discover evidence of a lost Golden Age. There was a rise of secret societies, nationalisms and new forms of Romanticism.

The exploration of non-rational aspects of life began to appear in the arts, literature, theology and philosophy. Magic, mythology, the paranormal, exotic cultures, ancient prophecies and the dream world became major areas of interest. By the late nineteenth and early twentieth century, psychologists such as Freud and Jung continued in the same vein. Their initial approaches to psychology were conventionally scientific. But later, their work was to take on a clear Romantic aspect as they ventured into the hidden and non-rational areas of human experience. In the twentieth century, transpersonal psychologists would follow and enhance the same Romantic quest.

The Appearance of Contradictions

The Enlightenment did produce unanticipated consequences. Paradoxically, several of these came from the work of theorists who had been driven by reason, only to reach radical conclusions. For example, in 1859, Charles Darwin published *On the Origin of Species*. Darwin's book outlined the idea of natural selection and the process of evolution. It contained meticulous observations of the natural world. These had led him to conclude that the morphology and behaviour of all living things, including human beings, had been determined by nature and not God. It's hard to imagine today how this claim shocked nineteenth-century sensibilities. People in every walk of life saw it as blasphemy. The unsettling part of this for religiously-inclined intellectual elites was that if it were blasphemy, it was one born of honest and reasoned inquiry. Science was beginning to challenge long-held assumptions about the nature of the world.

Opposition to political, social and religious orthodoxy was beginning to assist that process. The anti-Enlightenment trinity of Marx, Nietzsche and Freud used reasoned arguments to demonstrate that people weren't free agents who were able to pick and choose how they might negotiate the course of their lives. Hidden forces were at work, and these forces were of such elemental power that people had little control over them. For Marx, history was determined by economics. For Nietzsche, the social order was created by the tireless drivings of the will to power, and for Freud, people's destinies were forged from life by the unconscious. What all three theorists had in common was a belief that other realities were operating behind human intention. Their work suggested that progress wasn't something that could be achieved by simply getting rid of the traditional ways of doing things. Enlightenment aspirations of progress would always be largely frustrated. It was becoming clear that the Age of Reason wasn't going to be a wholly optimistic period, nor one with a shared vision of the future.

The New Humanism

The Enlightenment gave rise to new and diverse groups of humanists, who believed that social policies and the condition of people's lives should be guided not by God, but by humanity and its interests. Many humanists had been inspired by the work of Darwin, who was an agnostic and Marx, Nietzsche and Freud, who were atheists. But, the humanists proved to be far more influential in the development of transpersonal psychology than those who had inspired them. Their shift of perspective led to a systematic questioning of the *status quo*. Humanists began to undermine long-held assumptions about religious and social life and offered the possibility of establishing new ways of being human. This possibility introduced a subversive element to western thinking. It put paid to objective certainty and led, ultimately, to the development of transpersonal psychology.

The Emergence of Humanistic Psychology

By the twentieth century, humanists had increased in numbers and gained influential members. In 1967, Abraham Maslow, a psychologist, was named Humanist of the Year by the American Humanist Association. Maslow was a friend and colleague of Anthony Sutich, a psychologist who had an interest in mysticism. These psychologists had become increasingly troubled about the development of psychology after the second world war. Two psychological perspectives had come to dominate western psychology. These were psychoanalysis, which Maslow named the 'first force' of psychology. The other was behaviourism, which he named the 'second force' of psychology.

Sutich and Maslow were critical of psychoanalysis for several reasons. They objected to what they saw as Freud's acknowledgement of biological determinism, or the view that human nature is determined largely by biology. They also rejected Freud's pessimism. Freud seemed to be preoccupied with what was *wrong* with humanity. They thought he was overly concerned about madness, war, crime, conflict and the darker aspects of human nature, when he might have given equal consideration to the wonderful things humanity had achieved.

Sutich and Maslow objected to behaviourism on the grounds of its environmental determinism. Behavioural psychologists promoted the idea that people were as they were because of what they had been taught and what they had learned. They believed people were more or less passive recipients of environmental influences. Sutich and Maslow saw this as simplistic and as a total denial of other contributory elements of human development including human agency, existential dynamics and the operation of chance.

They felt neither of these perspectives recognised the radical potential of human agency. They believed both perspectives were pessimistic and failed to affirm human dignity. Sutich and Maslow were determined to break the stranglehold that psychoanalysis and behaviourism had on the academic world. They wanted to create a 'third force' of psychology.

The third force would be entirely different from the other two. It would follow the humanist principle of being human-centred and not biology- or environment-centred. It would adopt the distinction the Enlightenment philosopher, Immanuel Kant, had made between 'phenomena' and 'noumena.' Phenomena were appearances or how people perceived the world. Noumena were the realities behind appearances, not what people made of things, but the real nature of things. According to Kant, noumena would always be unknowable. Put simply, in their construction of the third force of psychology, Sutich and Maslow would take phenomena - *human experience* - as their primary focus. This new perspective would be called 'humanistic psychology.'

In 1958, Sutich and Maslow founded the *Journal of Humanistic Psychology*. Other psychologists were attracted to the development of humanistic psychology, including the highly influential psychoanalyst Otto Rank, the existential psychologist, Rollo May and the psychotherapist Carl Rogers. Rogers was another humanist, who would be named Humanist of the Year by the American Humanist Association in 1964.

Rank had worked with Freud, but after years of collaboration, he had begun to question some of Freud's ideas. In particular, he rejected Freud's biological determinism and declared that people had agency. He believed they could become creative heroes by shaping their own personalities and the course of their own lives.

Rank's ideas attracted May. Both had been influenced by the theologian and philosopher Søren Kierkegaard and by Nietzsche. May had been deeply interested in mythology, human subjectivity, human agency and the development of the will. This interest eventually led to him to explore humanism, though he never relinquished his commitment to theology. May had been at the Union Theological Seminary in New York City, where he had become the student and close friend of the theologian, Paul Tillich.

In later years, May and Tillich were to join Rogers at the Esalen Institute in California.

The Esalen had been founded in 1962 by psychologists Michael Murphy and Dick Price. It played a leading part in the development of the Human Potential Movement, the movement which sought to realise the vast, creative potential of human beings and enrich the entire social world. The Human Potential Movement was led principally by the humanistic psychologist, George Leonard. Its work arose out of the counterculture of the 1960s. It was a period which saw a growing rejection of conventional ways of life and a movement towards psychedelic culture. Counterculture introduced new ideas to the western world. Amongst these was an interest in eastern religion and philosophy, including yoga, Zen, Buddhism, Hinduism, Taoism and Transcendental Meditation. All these beliefs and practices were seen as routes to self-transcendence and to the capabilities this state conferred. During the same period, people such as Timothy Leary and Ram Dass were exploring the nature and value of altered states of consciousness produced by the use of psilocybin, mescaline, LSD and other psychoactive drugs. The Esalen workers investigated the potential of these countercultural developments as ways to achieve drug-induced mysticism and elevated states of consciousness.

The Contribution of Carl Rogers

Perhaps more than any other theorist, Rogers was responsible for publishing the first comprehensive account of humanistic psychology. His name is now synonymous with humanistic psychology. Rogers' early efforts were generally well-received. By the late 1960s, humanistic psychology had become influential throughout the world. It came to be heralded as the principal alternative to psychoanalysis and behaviourism. This was quite an achievement. In such a short space of time, and with convention ranged against him, Rogers had changed the course of psychological history.

Rogers' Enlightenment Influences

Several themes in humanistic psychology had recognisable Enlightenment and anti-Enlightenment lineages. Rogers demonstrated a Kantian position, as modified by Kierkegaard and Nietzsche when he wrote in 1959, 'There is no such thing as Scientific Knowledge.' There are, instead, 'only individual perceptions of what appears to each person to be such knowledge.'[149] Just as Sutich and Maslow had done before him, Rogers declared the 'fundamental predominance of the subjective.' He wanted humanistic psychologists to address the subjectivity of the person. He believed this was the key to unlocking human potential. Following earlier studies by Donald Snygg and Arthur Combs, Rogers named the subjectivity of the person, the 'phenomenal field.' By so doing, he recalled the distinction Kant had made between subjective *phenomena* and objective noumena.

By identifying the subjective as the primary objective of humanistic psychology, Rogers emphasised the necessity of addressing the

140

individual. This is often taken for granted when people think of psychological perspectives. However, the strategy has a history. The idea of the individual had its roots in the Protestant Reformation of the sixteenth century when organic or collective notions of society were beginning to give way to the notion of society as a collection of individuals each seeking their peace with God. In England, the idea had influenced Enlightenment thinkers such as the political philosopher, Thomas Hobbes and, the so-called Father of Liberalism, John Locke. In France, it had been adopted by François Quesnay, the leader of a group of free-trade economists called the Physiocrats. Their idea of 'economic individualism' informed philosophy and political theory and eventually, it became an orthodoxy of modern western thought.

Rogers' Anti-Enlightenment Influences: The Influence of Nietzsche

Nietzsche's work was highly influential in the development of humanistic psychology. Rogers adopted Nietzsche's concept of the will to power in the form of a 'basic tendency and striving - to actualize, maintain and enhance the experiencing organism.'[150] Rogers believed this basic tendency propelled individuals, or at least some individuals, towards a state of 'self-actualization.' According to Rogers, this state was the pinnacle of human achievement. The term 'self-actualization' was first used by Maslow, who had been inspired by Nietzsche's notion of the *Übermensch* or the Overman. The *Übermensch* was the state of human perfection described in Nietzsche's seminal work, *Thus Spoke Zarathustra.* [151]

The most striking aspect of humanistic psychology that owes itself to Nietzsche's work can be seen in Rogers' account of how subjectivity operates. There is a clear parallel between Nietzsche's description of the psyche and the one proposed by Rogers. In *The Will to Power*, Nietzsche refers to the psyche as an unknowable complexity, an abundance of contrary drives and impulses that can be brought to a harmonious totality by an organising idea which forms the centre of the psyche. This organising idea is how the psyche achieves its 'heroic goal,' the authentic self. Once achieved, the self gives meaning to life.

Rogers' model describes the psyche as an unknowable complexity crowned by a regulating 'self.' The self is the product of a subjective 'I' and an objective 'me.' The I represents the person's inner experiences and reflections. The me is made up of how the person is habitually defined by others, for example, as old, even-tempered or intelligent. The self is an emergent property; it's completely different from the two processes which inform it. Once formed, it becomes the executive of the psyche, and, according to Rogers, it has two characteristics. The first is that it unites a relatively stable set of ideas people have about themselves, a sense of selfhood. The second is that it tries to regulate conflicting impulses within the psyche. Its task is to establish a balance and achieve a working harmony. Rogers calls this harmony, congruence. Congruence is established when a person's sense of self is the same as what they believe to be the way they ought to be, their ideal self. If that happens, the person achieves self-actualisation. They reach a state of authenticity, health and full capacity to engage with life.

An important and much-overlooked aspect of the self is that it's not simply the same thing as personality. All too often, psychologists and laypeople see personality as something a person *has;* it's thought of as unitary and fixed. But the self isn't unitary; it's the product of a daily negotiation between the person and others. Consequently, it isn't fixed; it can change, and it can change for the better. The concept of self is an embodiment of Enlightenment values: it's inherently optimistic, it offers the possibility of progress through the application of reason.

Rogers' Anti-Enlightenment Influences: The Influence of Freud

Rogers was a trained psychoanalyst and recognised the value of Freud's concept of the unconscious. Freud had inherited from Nietzsche the idea that the unconscious was ultimately unknowable. That posed a problem. How could Freud study something that was outside consciousness and is unknowable? To solve the problem, he used a distinction theologians had come up with when they reflected upon the nature of a God who was held to be unknowable. Freud proposed that whilst it wasn't possible to *know of* the unconscious directly, it was possible to *know about* the unconscious indirectly. For example, he could look at its various manifestations in a person's dreams or in their neurotic symptoms. Freud's strategy was largely successful, but in later years, Rogers thought it was unnecessary. He argued that whilst there would always be unknowable unconscious influences in people's lives, it would make better sense to accept their presence and then ignore

143

them. If therapeutic success was to be achieved, it was essential to attend to those matters that *were* knowable and which, therefore, could be worked on directly. Therapy should always be based upon pragmatism and optimism. Progress would then be possible. The patient, or as Rogers preferred to have it, 'the client,' would not only be fully involved with the therapeutic process but they would also be able to *participate* in securing an agreeable outcome.

Other Influences: The Influence of Theology

At the Union Theological Seminary, Rogers became familiar with the Greek term *agapé*. Agape appears throughout the *New Testament*, and it means love. It refers to love not like *eros*, which means erotic love, or to *philia*, which means kindred love. Agape refers to unconditional charitable love. Rogers knew that agape was the term used in the *New Testament* to describe the love of God for his children. It was also used to refer to the love of his children for God and one another. It was the kindest love people could have for their children and dearest ones. It was the love a priest should have for the people in his care; it was the love observed in the Confessional. Over the centuries it had proved its worth for that purpose. With that in mind, Rogers adopted the idea of agape and incorporated it into the therapy that would be employed by humanistic psychology and which came to be known as, client-centred, and later, person-centred therapy. To avoid any exclusive religious associations, he renamed agape, 'unconditional positive regard.'

Rogers used several aspects of auricular or spoken and heard confession to develop person-centred therapy. He believed an agreeable outcome to therapy required the observation of a particular kind of relationship between the therapist and the client. The therapist had to practise the so-called three core values of person-centred therapy. These values were empathy, unconditional positive regard and genuine warmth; and all three were derived from Rogers' understanding of how auricular confession worked.

Not surprisingly, Rogers' person-centred therapy found favour with faith groups who saw it as a progressive force for good. Some faith groups adopted it to serve the psychological, as well as the spiritual, needs of their members. It lent itself to that purpose because it's relatively easy to understand and doesn't require extensive training. It can also be modified to suit the particular needs of those who want to use it. Some of these groups saw aspects of person-centred therapy as being agreeably compatible with their faith without ever realising that both had a common source.

The Appeal of Humanistic Psychology

From the beginning, it was clear that a distinctly democratic principle informed Rogers' enterprise. It was a change of emphasis that was bound to appeal to American intellectual sensibilities. American culture was thoroughly imbued with the liberal, optimistic outlook of John Locke, who had stressed the equality of every individual before God. Therefore, he came to be regarded as the champion of the oppressed. The first settlers in the Americas were the dispossessed, the religious and political refugees, buccaneers, bandits and adventurers, the orphans, the poor, the unwanted and rootless souls. These people carried Lockean ideas with them. Through their influence, ideas of equality, freedom and progress - all Enlightenment values - were enshrined in the American Declaration of Independence and guided the shaping of the new nation. This point is important. If humanistic psychology was to be accepted and thrive in America, it had to present itself as compatible with the American Dream. The dream was, of course, the unshakeable belief that in the New World, success would be within reach of everyone. Rogers' principles were in line with the American Dream, and this would do much to smooth the way of humanistic psychology into the American way of life. Since America was the centre of world psychology, what was likely to impress American psychology was likely to influence the world.

Criticisms of Humanistic Psychology

a)The Claim that Humanistic Psychology is not Scientific

Humanistic psychology wasn't always critically well-received. There were psychologists and others who were quick to point out that it was not scientific. Their objections usually involved claims that the basic concepts of humanistic psychology were vague, over-simple, inconsistent, and therefore, not measurable. However, this is also the case with other psychological perspectives. For example, in social psychology, the term 'group' has *dozens* of definitions, and yet social psychology still operates successfully. In analytic psychology, the term 'archetype' is not always used consistently, nor it can be measured; yet it's in daily use throughout the psychological world.

Critics have also claimed that humanistic psychology isn't scientific because it isn't based upon experimentation or some other systematic collection of data. Consequently, they believe it shouldn't be taken seriously and dismiss its findings out of hand. Objections of this kind are simply fallacious. They assume there's only one way of doing science and that way is nomothetic science - the kind of science based upon causal analysis and which is used in much of the natural sciences. Not only is this claim untrue, but it also demonstrates ignorance about other, equally time-honoured, branches of science. Nomothetic science tries to investigate things objectively. It uses measures and experiments to test hypotheses and offer explanations. However, the tradition of science known as hermeneutics does not use measurements or experiments, nor does it offer explanations. It approaches things diagnostically and operates in the same way as archaeologists, astrophysicists, physicians and pathologists. By using forensic reconstruction and interpretation, hermeneutic scientists *try to make sense of what they're investigating and so create understanding.*

In the main, humanistic psychology uses a hermeneutic approach. It addresses subjectivity, and, by its very nature, subjectivity isn't directly observable. Subjectivity is not a thing. It can't be seen or videoed. Nor is subjectivity in any way uniform and discrete. It's subtle, ambivalent and often confused. It isn't possible to measure something that isn't directly observable, and which is subtle, ambivalent and often confused. Without measurements, experiments can't be carried out, and without experiments, predictions and then explanations can't be made. However, it's entirely possible *to think about* subjectivity. It can be examined by conceptual analysis and in terms of that, subjectivity can be interpreted. An interpretation of something doesn't lead to an explanation; it enables an *understanding* of it, which can then be evaluated. That's precisely what humanistic psychology sets out to do. It can make substantial inroads into understanding human subjectivity and how it relates to behaviour. It follows that this successful approach to the study of the subjective worlds of people can't be legitimately criticised for not using the methods of nomothetics.

b) The Claim that Humanistic Psychology is Biologically Blind

Dennis Wrong believed the model of the person employed by humanistic psychology is flawed. He thought humanistic psychologists begin with a one-dimensional model of what people are like before they set about studying them and it's an environmentally one-dimensional model at that. The humanistic psychological model of the person doesn't take into account genetics, brains, and other biological factors. Rogers had buried the body. Therefore, humanistic psychology promotes what Wrong has called an 'oversocialized conception' of the person.[152] Their perspective is partial, simplistic and possibly dangerous. Wrong believed it had no place in modern psychology.[153]

Objections of this kind are spurious. At first sight, they might seem plausible, but closer analysis suggests they're not. Rogers wouldn't deny the role biological factors play in determining human social behaviour and experience. Indeed, he could reject Wrong's criticism by referring to the perceptions he shared with his former student, Eugene Gendlin, whose concept of the 'felt sense' or the bodily feel of clients' problems, has become a universally recognised therapeutic site of investigation.[154] Several other forms of embodied psychotherapy emerging from humanistic psychology have also been established.[155]

Humanistic psychology occupies an altogether different focus of analysis to that of biology. Human nature can be studied legitimately at biological, cultural and psychological focuses of analysis without having necessary recourse to one another. Rogers wanted to construct a perspective that would examine, as it were, psychological software and not hardware. It was intended to look at the mind and not the brain, meaning and not synapses and volition and not reflexes.

c) The Claim that Humanistic Psychology is a Sanction for Selfishness

Humanistic psychology was thought by some psychologists, such as Michael and Lise Wallach, to be yet another manifestation of what they called, 'psychology's sanction for selfishness.' With the advent of humanistic psychology, they felt 'the advice to liberate ourselves had become extreme' and, for humanistic psychologists, 'the greatest good was fidelity to [the] self and its development.'[156]

Their fear was that very idea of selfhood could promote excessive self-interest and diminish social concern. Individual rights might even begin to take precedence over social responsibilities, and a self-interested generation could emerge.

In recent times, it's undeniably the case that self-interested generations have emerged throughout the world. Evidence of this can be seen in its various manifestations, including the steep rise of involvement with national, regional, political and sexual identities, gender transitioning, cosmetic surgery, social media, as well as researching ancestry 'to find out who you really are.' Some commentators in the popular press have referred to 'the rise of selfism,' 'generation selfie' and 'generation of the self-obsessed' to make the point.

However, it would be simple-minded to pin the rise of a self-interested generation on psychology and especially, humanistic psychology. After all, to a lesser or greater extent, all the modern social sciences are interested in human subjectivity. So too, are branches of biology, electronics, robotics, computing and artificial intelligence, architecture and medicine. Some of the greatest insights into human subjectivity are ancient. Down the ages, theology, philosophy, history, art, literature and drama have made perceptive insights into human subjectivity without producing the self-interested generations we see today. It seems, therefore, that an interest in subjectivity is widespread, and it's always been based upon our curiosity about what makes us the way we are. The deeper cultural processes that have produced the present global interest in self-life are, no doubt, complex and will be the subject of a proliferating social scientific inquiry in the years ahead.

d) The Claim that Humanistic Psychology Fails to Address the Dark Side of Humanity

In its attempt to make sense of human life, humanistic psychologists and especially Rogers attracted criticism from within its own ranks. May pointed out that humanistic psychology was naive.[157] Rogers was committed to the idea that humanity 'is basically good,' May felt this was an irresponsible assertion and quoted the theologian, Martin Buber's more plausible claim that humanity 'is basically good *and evil.*' This correction would bring humanistic psychology in line with those of its originating influences from the likes of Marx, Freud, Nietzsche and Jung.

May had a point, but so did Rogers. Having studied at one of the finest theological seminaries in the world, Rogers knew a thing or two about good and evil. His claim wasn't that people were *exclusively* good, nor did he deny evil. He once remarked that he looked at people optimistically. But that remark wasn't naive; it was intended to frame the client-therapist relationship. It was a mantra for practice which works well. He knew there was virtue in appealing to the good that was inherent in people not only during the therapeutic process but generally, in everyday life. (Rogers' belief is not unlike the Quaker conviction that people should 'seek that of God' in everyone. When the divinity inherent in a person's humanity, is nourished with love, it will result in the flourishing of all.)

e) The Claim that Humanistic Psychology is Uncritical

Critical psychologists such as Ian Parker[158] and Isaac Prilleltensky[159] have raised criticisms that aren't so easily dismissed. One of their principal objections is that humanistic psychology places too much emphasis upon individual experience. In their various ways, critical psychologists have argued that when people have problems which are sufficient to make them seek professional help, it's a grotesque mistake to think they're struggling with some sort of inner incongruence. It's more likely the case that these people are casualties of a political, economic or domestic system, which is ruining their lives. A person's distress isn't because they have a disordered self, it's a result of their constant exposure to the corrosive effects of inequality, poverty, ignorance, exploitation, abuse within the family, alienation, ill-health and death.

For this reason, Robert Shaw and Karen Colimore regard humanistic psychology as an elitist exercise in which the generally well-off find a way of becoming generally better off. At best, it's an unwitting upholder of the *status quo*, and at worst, it serves ideological purposes as an instrument of control.[160]

Humanistic psychologists, along with most other psychologists, are all too familiar with their work being labelled 'psychologism.' The term is used pejoratively. It means work that attempts to make sense of non-psychological phenomena using the language of psychology and failing to achieve anything of value. Psychologists are aware of this danger. When it becomes clear that powerful social influences bear upon psychological theory, or more usually, therapeutic practice, they're generally alerted to it and adjust accordingly. An example of this is Erich Lindemann and Gerald Caplan's introduction of crisis intervention therapy beginning in the 1940s. When a person undergoing therapy was judged to be well enough to return to their usual way of life, consideration would be given to the possible toxic nature of that way of life. Interventions would then be made to lessen or overcome the risk of a return to a context-induced state of distress. That might prevent the need for yet more therapeutic referrals.[161]

Nevertheless, critical psychologists have a point. Humanistic psychologists cannot claim to address the entirety of the human condition with all the distress life involves. Humanistic psychology is partial, and it can be politically and socially naive. If it is to be a useful instrument in the toolbox of life-fixes, then humanistic psychology will have to integrate with broader and more radical approaches to social engineering. (Precisely which ones for that purpose could provide PhD students with endless opportunities) Even so, whilst this realisation indicates a major limitation of humanistic psychology, paradoxically, it also highlights its strength.

If humanistic psychological and radical approaches to human engineering are contrasted, the full potential of humanistic psychology can be seen. Imagine a world where, through radical intervention, poverty, oppression, and injustice had been eliminated and where opportunities were open to all. Would people's lives then be carefree and emptied of all existential concerns? The answer to this question has to be no. People would still have to cope with the day to day demands of their everyday lives: birth trauma, illness, sibling rivalry, bullying, failure at school, falling in love, failure in love, the birth of children, betrayal, divorce, grief, confusion, occupational disappointments and the prospect of death. These, largely unavoidable, biographical events inevitably produce experiences of anxiety, fear, love, joy, frustration, anger, regret, jealousy and hopelessness. A look back at history shows these are what ordinary people experience throughout their lives. No matter what their position is in society and no matter which social, political, economic or cultural circumstances prevail at the time, they'll still experience a kaleidoscope of testing emotions. *This rich, bewildering, confusion of emotions provides the ground and the entire rationale for the role humanistic psychology has to play and underlines its purpose and value.*

It's evident, therefore, that the limitations of humanistic psychology at a societal level of analysis don't rule out its value at the level of individual analysis. Conversely, the value of humanistic psychology at an individual level of analysis doesn't rule out the value of broader and more radical perspectives at a societal level of analysis. These are not mutually exclusive activities; they're simply *convenient, analytically separable* ways of looking at things. If used imaginatively, each can integrate and enhance the other in our attempts to make sense of human life.

The Emergence of Transpersonal Psychology

The claim that humanistic psychology is able to address

circumstances and emotions that attend every generation leads us neatly to how transpersonal psychology came into being. For it was the final and most telling criticism of humanistic psychology by humanistic psychologists themselves that led to its development.

In an article published in 1976 titled, 'The Emergence of the Transpersonal Orientation: A Personal Account'[162] Sutich tells us that during two seminars on Humanistic Theology at the Esalen Institute in 1966, an unseemly dispute broke out regarding mystical experience as a legitimate object of psychological study. At one of these seminars, Sutich had asked, 'Has anyone ever had a mystical or similar experience?' The answer had been no. Sutich, Maslow, Murphy and several others saw spirituality as an integral aspect of human development and ultimately, of human health. They were convinced it had been neglected and should be studied. However, in a later seminar, their views were openly opposed by several of those present. One of the main antagonists was Friedrich Perls. Perls was a Jewish-Zen Buddhist psychoanalyst whose influence on humanistic psychology, and especially on Sutich, had been profound. The mocking opposition of this authoritative figure in the humanistic psychology movement might account for Maslow's and Sutich's extreme reaction.

The dispute was of such intensity that it caused Sutich and Maslow to question their continuing commitment to the movement. Sutich wrote, [Humanistic psychology] 'did not adequately accommodate the depths of the cultural turn toward the 'inner-personal' world or give sufficient attention to the place of men in the universe or cosmos.'[163] By 1967, after extensive correspondence and meetings between Maslow, Sutich, the psychoanalyst Stanislav Grof, and others, Maslow was moving towards a position where he felt able to declare the 'fourth force' of psychology. Initially, this came in the form an address to a meeting at the Unitarian Church in San Francisco titled, 'The Farther Reaches of Human Nature.' The address developed some of the ideas in *The Psychology of Science* that he had published in the previous year. It had railed against the self-privileging nomothetic version of scientific inquiry, and promoted the exploration of human experience.[164] In the San Francisco address, Maslow went further. The well-attended meeting heard his plans for a psychology of transformation. It would be a psychology that would recognise transcendental realms beyond self-actualisation. The attainment of these would be the bouquet of human life. In the published version of the San Francisco address, he wrote, 'We need to teach our children unitive perception, the Zen experience of being able to see the temporal and the eternal simultaneously, the sacred and the profane in the same object.' [165] In this single iconic sentence, Maslow laid bare the absolute goal of his fourth force in psychology.

Transpersonal Psychology

The idea of transcendence was basic to Maslow's venture. He wanted to raise:

... the wise, self-actualizing, old adult who knows the whole ... of the world, all its vices, its contentions, poverties, quarrels, and tears, and yet is able to rise above them, and to have the unitive conscious

156

in which he is able to see ... the beauty of the whole cosmos, in the midst of all the vices, contentions, tears and quarrels. Through defects, or in defects, he is able to see perfection.[166]

Both Maslow and Sutich struggled to find a suitable name for their fourth force in psychology. At first, they were impressed by the innovation of Julian Huxley (another of the American Humanist Association's Humanist of the Year in 1962) who coined the term, Transhumanism, to refer to the active betterment of humanity using science and technology. Hence, their initial formulation was 'Transhumanistic Psychology.' In 1967, the term 'transpersonal' appeared for the first time in an article written by Sutich. It set out an ambitious manifesto:

The emerging "Fourth Force" is specifically concerned with the study, understanding, and responsible implementation of such states as being, becoming, self-actualization, expression and actualization of meta-needs (individual and "species-wide"), ultimate values, self-transcendence, unitive consciousness, peak experiences, ecstasy, mystical experience, awe, wonder, ultimate meaning, transformation of the self, spirit, species-wide transformation, oneness, cosmic awareness, maximal sensory responsiveness, cosmic play, individual and species-wide synergy, optimal or maximal relevant interpersonal encounter, realization and expression of transpersonal and transcendental potentialities, and related concepts, experiences and activities.[167]

By and large, this statement of intent still stands today. It epitomises the purpose of transpersonal psychology and defines its brief, and it was a brief that would inevitably attract the derision of other, more conventional psychologists.

The title 'transpersonal psychology' was adopted, and its entry into the professional world of psychology began. In 1969, Maslow, Sutich and Grof launched the *Journal of Transpersonal Psychology*. In the United States, this was followed by the founding of the Association of Transpersonal Psychology in 1972 and in 1978 the International Transpersonal Psychology Association in California and later San Diego in 1980. The international association was founded by Grof and held its first conference in Iceland during the following year. In 1975, Robert Frager and James Fadiman established a graduate training centre, the California Institute of Transpersonal Psychology, later called Sofia University. The *International Journal of Transpersonal Psychology Studies* was launched in 1981. The Institute of Mindfulness and Transpersonal Psychology was formed in 2011 to serve a global community. In the United Kingdom, the Transpersonal Psychology Section of the British Psychological Association was founded in 1996, and the *Transpersonal Psychology Review* was published soon after.

Since these early events, there has been a steady proliferation of transpersonal psychological studies. These include explorations of altered states of consciousness, creativity, anomalous experiences, for example out of the body and near-death experiences, lucid

dreaming, folklore, prayer, meditation, mindfulness, prophecy, transpersonal anthropology, parapsychology, transpersonal emotions such as love and compassion and the perception of time and eternity. Transpersonal psychologists have also pioneered novel approaches to psychotherapy such as guided visualisation, journaling or expressive writing and breathwork.

Transpersonal Psychological Approaches to Study

Transpersonal psychology has adopted an eclectic range of approaches to study. It accommodates both conventional and unconventional theoretical perspectives. Its practitioners employ the experimentation and surveys of nomothetics, as well as the projective tests and symbology of hermeneutics. Transpersonal studies also make use of meditation, psychonautics (deep self-exploration during altered states of consciousness) numerology, astrology, tarot and I Ching, from which revealed psychological content can be derived. It uses poetry, ritual and art through which revealed psychological content can be expressed.

Transpersonal Psychology Today

Whilst the centre of transpersonal psychological activity is to be found in the United States, and especially in California, it's gained a footing in Australia, the United Kingdom and elsewhere in Europe. Nevertheless, it remains on the margins of acceptability amongst conventional psychologists around the world.

Criticisms of Transpersonal Psychology

a) General criticisms

Since its inception, transpersonal psychology has received a great deal of criticism. Much of the criticism that has been directed towards humanistic psychology has also been directed towards transpersonal psychology: its concepts are vague; it isn't scientific, and it promotes selfishness. The response of transpersonal psychologists to these criticisms is much the same as those made by humanistic psychologists to their critics.

Transpersonal psychologists have also defended themselves against the criticism that transpersonal psychology is biologically blind. Ken Wilber helped to pioneer transpersonal psychology, and later, came to promote 'integral theory.'[168] He was at pains to point out that it's essential to integrate biological as well as transcendental lines of inquiry to address the human condition in its fullness. By so doing, he refuted those critics who claimed that transpersonal psychology is biologically blind and a sanction for selfishness. His integral theory also required transpersonal psychology to become involved with social and political issues.

Wilber offered a convincing reply to critics who had suggested that transpersonal psychology had failed to address the dark side of human nature. His work emphasised the importance of engaging in 'shadow work.' Shadow work is the self-examination of those hidden aspects of the psyche that are corrupting but still formative of subjectivity. It's a necessary step towards the achievement of an authentic, richer and a fully-functioning life.

Michael Daniels has turned to Jung to make the same point and to address the criticism that transpersonal psychology is socially and politically naive. In his book, *Shadow, Self, Spirit*, Daniels introduces

160

a chapter titled, 'Towards a Transpersonal Psychology of Evil.' In it, he provides a comprehensive account of evil and suggests how transpersonal psychology can be employed not only to make sense of evil but also transcend it. Another chapter is titled, 'The Shadow in Transpersonal Psychology.' It outlines what he suggests is a 'mature, responsible, socially, politically and spiritually aware approach to the problem of evil, whether it exists in ourselves or in the activities of others.'[169] In this respect, he refers explicitly to the sexual, emotional and physical abuse of children, the activities of Satanist groups, along with the rise of racist, fascist and terrorist organizations that claim spiritual or transpersonal authority.

It's demonstrable, then, that transpersonal psychology hasn't failed to address the biological aspects of the human condition, the problem of evil and the political context of everyday life. Transpersonal psychologists have done so honestly and, without equivocation. Criticisms to the contrary are therefore erroneous.

b)The Claim that Transpersonal Psychology is Preoccupied with Mysticism and Religion

Albert Ellis, was a humanist and the founder of rational emotive behaviour therapy, an early form of cognitive behavioural therapy. In his 1989 article, 'Dangers of Transpersonal Psychology: A Reply to Wilber,' Ellis objected to what he saw as transpersonal psychology's unhealthy preoccupation with mysticism and religion.

He wrote: ... thinkers and psychologists who hold transpersonal or

161

transcendental ideas do not *necessarily* but very *often* promulgate almost exactly the kind of absolutistic ideology that is devoutly held by the religious and political sectarians who may some day atomically annihilate the whole human race.[170]

This is a rather puzzling criticism from a psychologist whose work is respected throughout the world. Not only does it harbour a partial and indeed, a rather feckless view of religion, but also, it suggests that transpersonal thought is potentially *dangerous*. But if transpersonal psychology is dangerous, it's a danger only to the defensive certainty of those who would deny the spiritual lives of others.

Ellis's view that transpersonal psychology has a *preoccupation* with mysticism and religion is equally puzzling. It's akin to criticising cognitive psychology for having a preoccupation with cognitive processes or behavioural psychology for having a preoccupation with behaviour. Perhaps Ellis's objection tells us more about his general aversion to religion than it does about the nature of transpersonal psychology.

c) The Claim that Transpersonal Psychology Lacks a Clear Focus

May, whose early influence on the development of transpersonal psychology was profound, also had reservations, which later he chose to withdraw. Amongst these was the claim that transpersonal psychology had blurred the real distinction between religion and psychology. Psychology should not be about transcendent matters. Rather, it should be about the pressing developmental concerns in everyday life. Not only was transpersonal psychology becoming blinkered to the wider aspects of personhood, but also, it had become a mish-mash of eccentric theoretical developments that lacked a legitimate psychological basis.[171]

There's something to be said for these observations. Early transpersonal psychology was undoubtedly philosophically naive. The humanistic psychologist, Eugene Taylor, suggested that its emphasis on the transcendent tended to lift it beyond rationality to the point where it had become anti-intellectual.[172] Taylor was probably right. However, those involved with the development of transpersonal psychology did broaden their concerns to include the wider aspects of personhood that May and others had suggested were lacking in early expressions of transpersonal psychology.

Transpersonal psychology may well have become a mish-mash of eccentric theoretical developments, but then the same is true of other established psychological perspectives such as social psychology and psychoanalysis. That has not stopped these

perspectives from prospering. The labels we place on various forms of psychological study don't point to strictly defined and exclusive regimes but instead they indicate general areas of interest and their associated methods.

The claim that transpersonal psychology lacks a legitimate

psychological basis is spurious. It depends on how one defines 'legitimacy' and how one defines 'psychological basis.' Only those who are convinced of their own righteousness in these matters can find justification in such a claim.

d) Criticisms made of Transpersonal Psychology by Humanistic Psychologists

Some criticisms of transpersonal psychology have come from humanistic psychologists. For example, in his paper, 'The Deified Self: A "Centaur" Response to Wilber and the Transpersonal Movement,' Kirk Schneider took exception to the work of Wilber, and by implication, to 'many others who side with the transpersonal movement in psychology.' He suggested that some of the central concepts Wilber had explored in his integral theory lacked plausibility. His ideas had little relevance to the modern world. In particular, Schneider thought the notion of 'ultimate consciousness' was highly problematic. He argued that a world characterised by a transcendent state of ultimate consciousness would cease to be recognisably human. It was the very boundaries and conflicts in human life that gave it its richness. The peaks and troughs of life's course were sources of its revivifying potential. Schneider wrote:

[Without these contrasts we] might foster generations of persons who would no longer know joy because they had forgotten sorrow; who would no longer value love because they had forgotten commitment; which would no longer question life because they had forgotten how to think critically and who would no longer feel impassioned because they had forgotten struggle and strife.[173]

Schneider is right, of course, but his criticisms are laid more appropriately at the door of Wilber's integral theory than they are at transpersonal psychology. In any case, it's arguable that Schneider has misunderstood the use of such terms as 'transcendence' and 'ultimate consciousness' in transpersonal psychology. These terms are what the sociologist, Max Weber would call 'ideal types.' They don't represent real things; they're idealisations. An idealisation is a model definition of something; it allows comparison and analysis of particular versions of it when they occur in everyday life. In other words, the terms Schneider objected to, are used *because they enable the analysis of things that people experience.*

Conclusion

Transpersonal psychology has been several centuries in the making, and despite the contrary claims of conventional schools of psychological thought, it's finally come of age. It's a necessary development. It's beginning to eclipse the secularist assumptions of those psychological perspectives that flourished in modernity, but which are now becoming estranged to the postmodern world.

Transpersonal psychology addresses the very soul of humanity. And indeed, in this way, it's true to the very name of psychology. In literal terms, psychology means 'talking about the soul.' Addressing the soul directly and without embarrassment, can lead to a transformation of lives and a transformation of a kind not afforded by most other psychological perspectives. This transformation can bring salvation to a world shocked by a new awareness of the precariousness of life on earth. It can give guidance to people who have lost confidence and clear direction. Transpersonal psychology offers the possibility of illuminating the spiritual grounds of human resilience. It aims to bring psychological respectability to the study of spirituality and to give life by restoring to our collective consciousness the grace lost in time but remembered in eternity.

B. The Quaker Way

The children of God are not of this world, neither do they mind only the things of this world, but the things which are eternal …

George Fox, 1651

Introduction

The prospect before me is daunting. You might not know about the Quaker faith, and it's up to me to describe it. I want to do that well and give you a clear account, but it won't be easy because there isn't a standard view of the Quaker way. You can be sure that whatever I write, someone, somewhere, will want to amend it. They'll think I've overstated something or I've not dealt sufficiently with an aspect of the faith they feel is important.

All isn't lost, however. The philosopher, Isaiah Berlin, has invented a helpful strategy for someone in my situation. After reading the fairy tale, *Cinderella*, Berlin noticed something. The glass slipper fitted Cinderella and nobody else. However, all the other characters still recognised it as a glass slipper. Berlin called this the 'Cinderella complex.' I'll cite the Cinderella complex here to support my efforts. Some Quakers might see any account of the Quaker faith I come up with as just my own, but they will still recognise it as a sincere attempt to get it right. With that in mind, I'll put my trust in Isaiah Berlin and carry on. Please bear with me, though. What I write here won't be an exhaustive account of the Quaker way of life; it'll only *indicate* what that usually involves.

Who Are The Quakers?

Let's start with one or two questions people often ask. One such is, 'Who are the Quakers?' Well, they're a religious group. They can be found in small communities in every corner of the world. The movement began in Britain, where they are now few in number. There are many more in North and South America and Africa. The Quaker faith has its roots in Christianity, but not all Quakers see themselves as Christians. Some Quakers see their faith as *arising out of Christianity but are not necessarily confined to it*. Some have joint membership with other religions. I've met Quakers who are also Anglicans, Methodists, Buddhists, Jews, Pagans, Muslims, Roman Catholics, Bahá'í, Hindus and people of no faith seeking direction. Why is this possible? It's because Quakers welcome anybody who wishes to join them in their services which are called meetings for worship.

Why Are They Called 'Quakers?'

In the beginning, Quakers referred to each other as 'Friends.' or as 'Friends of the Truth.' That was to change in 1650, when one of the early Quakers, George Fox, was brought before the magistrates in Derby. He was charged with 'the avowed uttering and broaching of divers blasphemous opinions contrary to a late Act of Parliament.' The magistrate, Gervase Bennett, asked Fox, 'What have you to say? Who are you? Why did you come here?' Fox replied, 'God moved us to do so and to tell thee that all thy preaching, baptism and sacrifices will never sanctify thee.

Look unto Christ and not unto men.' Bennett then said, 'You're demented, taken up in raptures. You speak too freely of God.' Fox was not going to be intimidated by a magistrate or anyone else for that matter. He replied, 'Tremble and quake at the name of the Lord!' Bennett was not impressed. He mused, 'You quake, do you? Quakers, eh?'[174] From that moment onwards, the name 'Quakers' came into use, firstly as a term of abuse and then, eventually, by the Quakers themselves. Today, their formal title is the Religious Society of Friends (Quakers). When I refer to them, though, I'll just call them Quakers.

Why Haven't I Heard Much About Quakers?

Some people have told me they haven't heard much about Quakers. That's probably because Quakers don't go out of their way to proselytise their faith. But they're around alright, and they've influenced, and continue to influence, many aspects of modern life. Let me explain.

In the early days, Quakers weren't allowed to go to universities by Acts of Parliament.[175] Since that meant they were effectively denied entry to the professions, many Quakers went into commercial life. They formed manufacturing companies such as the biscuit makers, Carr's and Huntley and Palmers, the matchmakers, Bryant and May, the glass makers Waterford Crystal and Clarks, the shoemakers. Friedrich Nietzsche's favourite tea-maker, Hornimans, was also a Quaker company! Quakers created confectioners such as Cadbury, Fry, Rowntree's and Terry's. All these companies made great efforts to set Quaker ways at the heart of their businesses. For that reason, they developed a reputation for integrity and fair dealing. Their faith made them successful, and their success led to other achievements.

For example, Quakers founded the State of Pennsylvania in the United States. They built theatres and created parks and gardens. They provided hospitals, such as Friends Hospital in Philadelphia and The Retreat in York. Towns such as New Earswick and Bourneville in England were built by Quakers. They founded educational settlements, schools, colleges, and universities, including the Friends' Theological College in Kenya, Johns Hopkins University in Maryland and the University of York (where the gowns are Quaker grey) in England. They helped to create Oxfam, the International Voluntary Service, Amnesty International, and Nike and Sony's multinational corporations.

Quakers established several charitable trusts such as the Barrow Cadbury Trust, the Sir James Reckitt Charity, Friends Provident Foundation, the Joseph Rowntree Foundation and Housing Trust, the Joseph Rowntree Charitable Trust and the Joseph Rowntree Reform Trust. These trusts are dedicated to rebalancing power in society by addressing twenty-first-century concerns about social inequalities, control and accountability, health and illness, peace and security, poverty and housing and green living.

What do Quakers believe?

What do Quakers believe? I should be able to answer that question easily enough, but what I say might surprise you. That's because there are no rules about what Quakers should or should not believe or what they should or should not do. Usually, religious groups have ways of declaring what they believe. They draw upon scriptures and other sources to justify their approach to religious and secular life. If I say the Quaker faith is a faith without rules, it will probably strike you as odd. But it's true. That's the way it is with Quakers. There's no Quaker rule book!

The Quaker Way

Quaker faith is not so much about believing certain things; it's more a guide about how to live a graceful life. How do they think this can be achieved? There are several points I might describe here. Firstly, Quakers hope to seek truth and guidance through a direct, dynamic personal relationship with God. They are content to remain uncertain about what God is. We're back to Berlin's Cinderella complex here. For Quakers, there is no single, widely accepted understanding of what God is. This has been true of the Judeo-Christian tradition generally. In medieval times, God had been referred to as a 'Cloud of Unknowing.' Meister Eckhart, speaks of taking leave of our ideas of God in order to find God. By that, he meant our images of God could replace God and lead to a form of idolatry. Modern theologians speak of the 'ineffable,' or that power beyond words to which they turn their thoughts and prayers. Each of us has an imperfect notion of God. Quakers recognise the value of other people's definitions of God without feeling the need to be constrained by them.

In any case, Quakers try to form their own disciplined, listening relationship to God without being confined to a set liturgy. How do they do this? They try to let their thoughts and actions be guided by what they feel the spirit of God is prompting them to do. Ultimately, this guidance comes out of the silence in their meetings for worship.

Quaker worship

How do Quakers worship? Quakers can meet for worship on any day of the week at any time. For practical purposes, they usually meet on Sundays when people have fewer occupational commitments. Quaker worship can vary in different parts of the world, but what they all have in common is that their worship is based on silence. There isn't a priest or someone who tells you what to do in Britain, and there's no order of service or other forms of structure. A meeting for worship is held at some allotted time. It begins when the first person sits down. Others join them and sit wherever they like. People are not required to do anything or think anything. It's sometimes the case, though, that someone might wish to take a problem they might have or thoughts of someone known to them to the meeting so that they may 'bring them into the light.' These meetings can be one of the few occasions when people can be themselves, unencumbered by the demands of their everyday responsibilities.

It might take a minute or two to settle down, but after a short time, the meeting will become 'gathered' in silence. A gathered meeting can be a wonderful experience. The silence is profound; you can hear a pin drop. In the depths of silence, the meeting often has a shared sense of itself. Peace and well-being enter in. Quakers use the beautiful seventeenth-century term, 'being centred down,' to describe what has happened.

The experience of being centred down will differ from person to person. Some people have described it as 'spiritual sunbathing.' They're able to reflect gently upon their lives and the things they care about. They seek and often find reassurance, inspiration and a sense of direction.

Others leave all thoughts of their everyday lives and go deep inside themselves, where they find what they say is a pure sense of being alive. For these people, time seems to stand still. The psychological distance between those present and loved ones elsewhere begins to dissolve. I've heard them describe this experience as coming home. It's a reunion. They return to their true source, where they can feel the love of the living and the dead.

If this sounds odd, then consider the words of the Catholic priest, John O'Donohue:

Sometimes the most important thresholds of mystery are places of silence. To be genuinely spiritual is to have great respect for the possibilities and presence of silence.[176]

He goes on to paraphrase Martin Heidegger:

… true listening is worship. When you listen with your soul, you come into rhythm and unity with the music of the universe.

Meister Eckhart described silence as 'the nearest thing to God.' And sometimes, in the depths of silence, people feel they are in communion with God. Silence can inspire people. They're close to their innermost thoughts, ideas form, connections are made, and insights arrive. The 'still small voice' within can be heard whispering from somewhere beyond thought. For some, it's the voice of God. The Sufi mystic Rumi knew this. He wrote, 'Silence is the language of God. All else is poor translation.'

Sometimes people are prompted to express what they have been given. When this happens, a Quaker will stand and speak or 'minister' to the meeting. Quakers might be moved in other ways to express themselves. I've heard people offer an unaccompanied folk song, a prayer or poem or play a piece on the piano. Whatever is said or done will be received gently by those around them. The ministry might not mean much to some people, but others will see it as a direct word of God. It might come as an answer to the very question they had taken to the meeting.

How should I summarise what Quaker meetings for worship are all about? If I were to use conventional theological language, I would say a Quaker meeting for worship is a celebration of awareness of our participation in the divine nature of God. Its gathered silence provides the spiritual tides of baptism, holy communion and eternal blessing. It's where Quakers find salvation through the peace that passeth all understanding.

Quaker Meeting Houses

Where do Quakers worship? Quakers can meet to worship anywhere. They don't have hallowed grounds especially sanctified for that purpose. For Quakers, everywhere on earth is sacred ground and is consecrated for worship. I've known Quakers meet during picnics on hilltops. They meet in schools, in people's houses, in prisons and factories. I've heard of a meeting for worship in the Garden of Gethsemane. However, Quakers do have Meeting Houses, and typically, that's where most of their meetings take place.

You'll have gathered by now that Quakers are unconventional in their approach to worship and to life itself. Their origins might be more than three centuries old, but they live their lives - their extraordinary and creative non-conformist lives - in ways that are sometimes surprisingly modern and sit well with many progressive ideas of the present age.

Quakers and Non-Conformity

In Paul's letter to the Romans, he wrote, 'be not conformed to this world.'[177] Paul's directive was clear. He was convinced that the ways of the world were corrupt. To conform to those ways was to endorse its corruption and take part in it. He implored Christians not to be conformed. Instead, they should be *transformed* into their true nature as children of God. They can do this by renewing their minds. This idea inspired the early Quakers, and it informed the way they approached life.

That's why Quakers don't always conform to social expectations. Conformity to beliefs and practices can provide people with a sense of direction in their lives. It can bring the rewards of security and achievement. But it can also constrain vitality and prevent spontaneity. Conformity can bring spiritual death. Quakers choose spiritual life. They have tried to free themselves from those constraints that so often accompany the desire for conformity.

The psychoanalyst, Karen Horney, referred to this restraining tendency of conformity as 'the tyranny of the should.'[178] She felt it important to point out that 'shoulds' can become psychological straight jackets in people's lives. They can also lead to debilitating anxiety and crush the spirit with guilt.

How Does This Non-Conformist Attitude Affect The Way Quakers Organise Themselves?

First of all, I should say that Quakers don't have strict 'shoulds,' nor do they have people in charge such as bishops and priests, who, in other religions, are guardians of their shoulds. Let me explain. It's usually the case that religions appoint people whose job it is to make sure their beliefs and practices are observed. These people are guardians of their faith. They can sanction members who don't conform to whatever orthodoxies the group has chosen to follow. Such arrangements are common enough. They can be found in religious and secular organisations around the world. The system usually works well, but unfortunately, it can be used to oppress people. We've all heard about people in positions of authority who have betrayed the trust people have placed in them. Quakers prefer to trust the promptings of love in their hearts and then make those promptings manifest.

James Nayler, one of the founders of Quakers, expressed this insight well. He wrote, 'My covenant is the new one, and the law in the heart, and here Christ is the rule of life to me for ever, and my law is spiritual and not moral.'[179]

Nayler meant that he denied the authority of kings, gentry, priests, texts, dogma and tradition, and the deadening constraints of 'carnal law', morality, social expectation, fear and desire. He regarded these as things of 'this world' and not of the spirit, and he believed their observance would lead only to a state of darkness. Nayler questioned why lives were governed by people who demanded that they should be lived in this way or that. He wanted a way of life governed by the gentle promptings of love in the hearts of people. He wanted people to seek truth inwardly through worshipful reflection.

That's why Quakers prefer not to have an ordained clergy. They are committed to the idea that nobody in their communities is of higher or lower rank or is closer to God than anybody else.

No matter who they are, everyone is a precious child of God and equal to all others.

However, Quakers do appoint people to organise their local Quaker communities. Arrangements differ slightly in Quaker communities around the world. In Britain, they have doorkeepers, tea-makers, librarians, representatives for various internal and external committees. They have notice readers, pastoral carers and people who take responsibility for the Quaker community's spiritual life. These people usually serve for three years and are then replaced by others.

Quakers have guiding principles that can help them to live fulfilled lives. These are laid out in a book called *Quaker Faith & Practice*.[180] The purpose of this book appears on the Quaker website. I quote from it: 'Quaker Faith and Practice is an attempt to express Truth through the vital personal and corporate experience of Friends. It is largely composed of extracts: a fitting way of expressing the breadth of Quaker theology. It also describes the current structures of Britain Yearly Meeting of the Religious Society of Friends.'[181]

Britain Yearly Meeting is the annual meeting of Quakers when they gather to determine how they might progress individually and collectively into the future. These guiding principles are not laid upon individuals as rules but as inspirations born of generations of Quakers' wisdom and insights. They are revised every few years as circumstances change.

Quaker Testimonies

It's been the practice to present Quaker values in terms of several Quaker Testimonies. These can vary slightly, but I'll adopt some of them here to outline what I believe to be the main themes of Quaker life. I'll present them in no particular order.

Equality

Quakers affirm the equality of all people, one with another, whether they are Quakers are not. The principle is at the heart of the Quaker way. It stems from the cherished commitment to the idea that there is 'that of God' in everyone. When I first heard this figure of speech, I thought it meant there was goodness in everyone. That might well be true, but it means far more than that. Quakers say everyone is blessed with an 'inner light' - a spark of divinity that unites us all and dignifies our common humanity. By acknowledging the reality of people's divinity, Quakers try to approach the people they meet *reverentially*. Sometimes, the inner light of certain people is hard to see, but it's always there. Quakers try to seek it out and then nourish it with love. When they do this, they believe people will respond. The inner light of a stranger is endowed by their very humanity. When it is genuinely acknowledged, it will increase and illuminate their place in the world.

This commitment to the equality of all can be seen in the way Quakers do things. For example, Quakers tend not to use personal titles - Mr, Mrs, Ms, Mx, and so on. Why is that? Well, titles convey status. They invite comparisons between *Lord* Smith, a title that might locate him high in the scheme of things, and *Miss* Smith, whose title might locate her lower in the scheme of things. If Lord Smith were to use his given name, *John Smith*, and Miss Smith used hers, *Joan Smith*, equality is established. They meet as equals and not as one who is in some way superior to the other. To some people, this arrangement might seem the stuff of modern liberal thought. When it emerged in the seventeenth century, however, it was revolutionary. And, in my view, it still is.

Conducting Business

A commitment to equality can also be seen in the ways Quakers do business. Quaker business meetings - to find direction about a pressing matter or formulate a policy for doing this or that - are held in the same way as meetings for worship. Business meetings begin with a period of silence. When those present have 'centred down' and they've reached the point of their deepest uncluttered humanity, the meeting can begin. People try to treat the matter for discussion and one another reverentially. They try to speak plainly, without artifice or rancour, to seek out the truth. When discussing and deciding upon policies or courses of action, Quakers don't vote. Why? They don't vote because if a vote is taken and the majority view is carried, then the views of all others present are ignored. The outcome isn't the outcome desired by everyone; it's the outcome desired by just *some* of those participating. Being in the majority doesn't make their views right.

Quakers say you must have the courage to acknowledge that you might be mistaken. The views of the outsider might be the direct word of God. Tolerance and respect for others and their ideas must be at the heart of Quaker decision-making. Instead of following the majority voice, Quakers seek to establish 'the sense of the meeting.' The sense of the meeting is something all those present can endorse. It might only be, 'We agree that we cannot reach a unified view of this matter. Therefore, we agree to continue to consider it prayerfully until a way forward can be discerned.' This process might slow down decision-making in the Board Room, but it's inclusive. It expresses humility and respect for the genuinely-held opinions and beliefs of those involved in trying to reach a decision and reverence for the spirit of God that guides each of them towards it.

Quaker Peace Testimony

Quakers came out of conflict. Although their kind had been in the making for centuries, it was in the 1640s when they first made an appearance recognisable today. It was a time of religious intolerance. Seemingly irreconcilable differences had emerged between the prevailing Christian denominations. Anglicans, Calvinists, Presbyterians, Independents, and Scottish Covenanters (all of whom came to be known as 'Puritans') were in bitter opposition to one another and to Roman Catholicism. All were convinced of their own claims to truth. Nothing was more important to them. They were prepared to live for, die for and indeed, kill for what they believed. They did so in great measure in the years which followed. Their self-righteous zeal led to witch hunts, torture, hangings, burnings and eventually, to the English Civil War and the spilling of blood on a scale unimaginable today.

In the uneasy peace which followed, the Quakers began to appear as a distinct group. The historian George Trevelyan wrote of them:

The Puritan pot had boiled over, with much heat and fury; when it had cooled and been poured away, this precious sediment was left at the bottom ... [The Quakers believed] Christian qualities matter much more than Christian dogmas. No church or sect had ever made that its living rule before. To maintain the Christian quality in the world of business and of domestic life, and to maintain it without pretension or hypocrisy, was the great achievement of those extraordinary people. England may well be proud of having produced and perpetuated them.[182]

Oliver Cromwell, the victorious Puritans' leader, didn't know what to make of Quaker people. They seemed to be a law unto themselves. They weren't receptive, nor were they afraid of his, or any other, worldly authority. Yet, they appeared to be a sincere and Godly people. It was an age of mistrust. Cromwell feared that Quakers might translate their aspirations to spiritual independence into armed insurrection. When he approached George Fox, a leading figure amongst Quakers, Cromwell asked for reassurance about their intentions. He got it. Fox wrote:

The next morning I was moved of the Lord to write a paper to the Protector, Oliver Cromwell; wherein I did, in the presence of the Lord God, declare that I denied the wearing and drawing of a carnal sword, or any other outward weapon, against him or any man; and that I was sent of God to stand a witness against all violence, and against the works of darkness; and to turn people from darkness to light; and to bring them from the causes of war and fighting, to the peaceable gospel.[183]

The world wasn't ready for that sort of testimony. People couldn't believe that Quakers wanted to establish peace on earth. But Quakers didn't just make statements; in the centuries which followed, they put their words into action. In the eighteenth century, they advocated peace during the War of Austrian Succession. They declared their commitment to peace during the Napoleonic Wars. Quakers raised £7,000, a large sum of money in those days, to provide relief for people whose lives had been uprooted by the war. Shortly afterwards, in 1816, they helped to found the Society for the Promotion of Permanent Peace (The Peace Society).

Quakers opposed the American Civil War, and many refused to pay taxes to finance the war or fines for their conscientious objection to it.

In 1864, Joseph Sturge led a Quaker mission to Tsar Nicholas in Russia to prevent the Crimean War. He was unsuccessful, but in the years that followed, he arranged relief for the Finnish people, who were starving as a result of the war.

In 1870, Quakers founded the Friends War Victims Relief Committee to help people distressed by the Franco-Prussian War. This committee continued its work into the twentieth century and in other theatres of war, including the South African War and the

First and Second World Wars. The Friends Ambulance Unit was founded in 1914 and served in conflicts around the world until the mid-twentieth century. Other Quaker organisations provided relief for people who had suffered in wars in Germany, Ireland, Spain, China, Japan, India, Gaza Strip, Korea, Vietnam and elsewhere.

Quakers have long been associated with a commitment to peace and peacemaking. It's true that some Quakers have joined the armed forces to contribute to what they felt were just causes. Many others have refused to do so. They have been unable to bring themselves to join in the process of inflicting death and injury on people who, like themselves, they regarded as children of God. In two World Wars, their refusal to bring harm to other human beings resulted in their being both admired and reviled. Some Quakers formed the Friends Ambulance Unit and served in front lines to help all those who needed them, whatever the colour of their uniforms. Quakers volunteered to work in hospitals at home and abroad. Some refused to do any war-related work. These conscientious objectors were imprisoned and often treated appallingly. In all this, Quakers held fast to their commitment to peace.

In 1947, the Quaker United Nations Office was founded. It operates in Geneva and the United Nations Headquarters in New York. Its purpose is to promote peace and justice through facilitation and quiet advocacy.

In that same year, the Religious Society of Friends was awarded the Nobel Peace Prize. It recognised the care and resettlement of refugees they had carried out before, during, and after the Second World War. Since that time, they've been used as trusted intermediaries in attempts to negotiate peace between warring factions throughout the world. They've brought to the attention of the United Nations matters relating to children soldiers, children and women prisoners, refugees and migrants, food security and climate change.

In 1936, Quakers attempted to bring otherwise overlooked matters to the British public's attention by publishing *Peace News*, a newspaper to serve and promote 'the grassroots peace and justice movement.'

In 1973, with funding from the Quaker Peace Studies Trust and the University of Bradford, Quakers established the Department of Peace Studies at Bradford. It was the first university department of its kind. It's now the world's leading university centre for the study of peace and conflict. Its first Professor of Peace Studies was the Quaker, Adam Curle. He subsequently carried out peacemaking activities in Zimbabwe, South Africa, the Balkans, Sri Lanka, Croatia and Northern Ireland.

After being approached by people in a New York prison, Quakers launched the Alternatives to Violence Project in 1975. The project attempts to find principled ways to address and overcome those conflicts which seem to be unavoidable aspects of modern life.

The AVP is now a global organisation. Quakers have introduced Turning The Tide, an initiative dedicated to promoting non-violent action for social change.

In 1978, British Quakers were at the forefront of forming the organisation, Conscience. This campaigning group advocates a progressive decrease in taxes paid for military purposes and a progressive increase in taxes paid to promote peace and peacemaking.

In 1994, the Joseph Rowntree Charitable Trust funded the establishment of a Peace Museum in Bradford. The museum's purpose is to explore 'the history and the often untold stories of peace, peacemakers, social reform and peace movements.'[184] In recent years, the museum has held exhibitions, workshops for schools, colleges and community groups. It's initiated research projects and made collaborative links with peace museums and other organisations around the world.

Quakers have established Peace Centres in Friends Meeting Houses and other places to offer information and outreach to local and regional populations worldwide. From these places and more centrally, they have promoted the cause of peace and raised support for peace and conflict-related local, regional, national and international issues.

Quakers were well-represented in the Greenham Common Women's Peace Camp in Berkshire, which saw them oppose the stationing of American offensive nuclear weapons in Britain. They have held regular meetings for worship outside RAF Menwith Hill near Harrogate, an air force base that provides communication and intelligence for NATO.

A desire for peace has been an aspect of Quaker faith that has sometimes led to their being held in contempt. Nevertheless, their efforts have achieved psychological and practical changes and have been of benefit to the world.

Love of the Created World

George Fox spoke of 'unity with the creation.' Modern Quakers speak of 'sustainability' and 'stewardship of the earth.' They can see there's that of God in all aspects of the created world.

In 1693, William Penn, the founder of Pennsylvania, expressed this sentiment so eloquently. He wrote:

> ... it would go a great way to caution and direct People in their Use of the World, that they were better studied and known in the Creation of it. For how could [they] find the Confidence to abuse it, while they should see the Great Creator stare them in the Face, in all and every Part thereof?[185]

We can illustrate this way of relating to the created world by looking at what the Jewish theologian Martin Buber wrote about relationships. In his 1923 book, *I and Thou*, he introduced what he called 'the philosophy of dialogue.'[186] By this, he meant that there were three distinct ways of relating to people. The first is when we

187

relate to someone lovingly. He called this an I-Thou relationship. The second is when we relate to someone simply as another human being, but without the presence of love. He called this an I-You relationship. The third is when we relate to someone who is perceived to be inhumane and beyond the pale. He called this an I-It relationship. He saw our relationship to God as between ourselves and the Eternal Thou. It's this relationship that should serve as a pattern for all others in our lives.

Buber extended his idea to refer to the natural world by considering our perception of a tree. Suppose we regard a tree merely as a source of building materials or as fuel or a provider of fruit and flowers. In that case, we enter into an I-It relationship with it. If we see a tree as a living organism with its own characteristics, we have an I-You relationship. But when we recognise the tree as divine, we create an I-Thou relationship with her. She becomes a manifestation of the mystery of life. The nature of our relationship with things determines how we treat them.

In the thirteenth century, Francis of Assisi demonstrated this perfectly. In his Letter to All the Faithful, we find him addressing the created world in terms of an I-Thou relationship. He refers to Brother Wind, Sister Water and Brother Fire. He addresses the earth as, 'Sister Mother Earth.'[187] He sees God's presence in what we might think of as the unlikeliest of places. In the *Sacra Commericium* and elsewhere, he speaks of 'Lady Poverty.'[188] Thomas of Celano tells us that shortly before Francis died, he called upon all creatures, including death, to praise God. He invited death to be his lodger with the words, 'Welcome, Sister Death.'[189] For Francis, all aspects of our experience of life, including its ending, should be recognised as manifestations of the Divine Spirit. It's clear that when Francis prayed, 'Thy will be done,' he meant it without exception. He saw the 'thou' in everything, and that determined how he lived his life, even unto death.

Meister Eckhart saw that too. For him, our spiritual birth is possible only when we can 'grasp God in all things.' In the sixteenth century, Ignatius of Loyola advised that rather than spending a long time in prayer, we should make an effort to find God in all things. In the *Take and Receive*, he wrote:

God dwells in all creatures: in the elements giving them existence, in the plants giving them life, in the animals conferring upon them sensation, in human beings bestowing understanding. So he dwells in me and gives me being ...[190]

My late friend, Guy Ragland Phillips, took that insight further. He saw the earth and the life it supports as manifestations of God. In his book, *The Unpolluted God*, he wrote:

Remember always: each tree has its spirit, each plant, each creature, each stream or pool or waterfall, each cave, rock and crag, each mountain and valley, each arm of the sea - all of these have their spirits as you have, and they are ready to respond to you.[191]

Phillips was a committed Quaker, but his writings have found a place in the hearts of modern British Pagans. Those avowed worshippers of the natural world recognise the illuminating presence of the Goddess in so much of what he had to say.

Phillips claimed all forms of 'Earthly cruelties,' such as deforestation, pollution of the rivers and seas, industrial mining and filling the skies with poisons, were sacrilege. In the 1960s and 70s, when much of the postwar western world enjoyed new-found prosperity, Phillips was one of the few people who dared to ask the question: Does our headlong pursuit of economic wealth justify our *despoiling of the earth*?

Quakers were quick to respond to Phillips's question. In 1971, they founded Greenpeace, the international organisation that seeks to 'ensure the ability of the Earth to nurture life in all its diversity,' by mounting campaigns against nuclear power, over-exploitation and pollution of the seas, deforestation, climate change and genetic engineering. Greenpeace hasn't been widely welcomed by nation-states and multinational corporations, which often see it as an obstacle to the creation of wealth. Even so, it continues to prove its worth. It's a source of education and a friend of others who dare to oppose those who would leave the earth bereft.

In 1975, Quakers played a leading part in creating the Ecology Party, a forerunner of the Green Party, which achieved success by having members elected to British and European Parliaments.

In 2011, Quakers launched the Canterbury Commitment. The commitment represents a recognition that climate breakdown is not simply environmental or physical. Rather, it's the direct result of global economic injustice. Climate change affects us all, but it does so unequally; some people are affected more than others. Worst affected are those who have lived sustainable lives for centuries and contributed least to climate breakdown. These people have seen their natural resources depleted and, in some cases, exhausted by powerful nation-states and multinational companies. Climate breakdown means that they now face drought, land erosion, famine, floods, extreme weather events, industrial-scale poisoning of rivers and seas, high mortality rates, and population loss. Yet, the people so affected have fewer resources, including political power, to do much about it. Therefore, it's clear that tackling this kind of inequality is fundamental to any initiative designed to bring justice and healing to the world.

At a gathering of Quakers from around the world in 2012, the Karabak Call for Peace and Justice was declared. The Call encouraged Quakers to secure climate justice, 'to be patterns and examples in a 21st-century campaign for peace and justice, as difficult and decisive as the 18th and 19th-century drive to abolish slavery.'

Since 2011, Quakers have worked with the Climate Justice movement. They've co-operated with campaigners worldwide to secure climate justice, and the economic transformation needed to achieve it. And as ever, they remain optimistic. They've come to see there is that of God in every situation. Even in the present ecological crisis, there is always the possibility of resurrection, of new growth. As Fox put it, we can be 'born afresh into creation.'

Seeking simplicity

Simplicity is a long-held Quaker value. Its significance can be explained in several ways. A superficial explanation is that it was a reaction of Quakers in the seventeenth century to people who dressed and acted flamboyantly. In popular parlance, these were called 'popinjays' - people who were far more concerned about showing off their wealth and standing in the community than they were about living godly lives. Quakers rejected this pretence, and by way of contrast, they insisted on dressing, acting and speaking moderately. They aspired to what T. S. Eliot called, 'A condition of complete simplicity. (Costing not less than everything)'[192] so that, in Fox's words, they could 'live adventurously, walking cheerfully over the world, answering that of God in everyone.'[193] Quakers still make a point of doing this.

There is a deeper reason for the Quaker value of simplicity. I can explain what I mean by outlining a distinction made by the psychoanalyst, Erich Fromm. He describes *having* and *being* as two distinct ways people can relate to the world. The difference between these two ways of experiencing life is fundamental.[194]

In the western world, people's lives are all too often geared towards the mode of having. There is widespread acceptance that having desirable things is a sign of success. The more one has, the more one is. Those who believe this display clothing, jewellery, cars, housing and membership of prestigious organisations to signal their achievements. It becomes a kind of fetish. Things are treated as objects of desire, not so much because of their designed utility, but for the social status and self-satisfaction, their possession bestows.

But chasing after possessions misdirects our gaze. Not only does living by having draw heavily upon the earth's resources but also it deforms human sensibilities and leads to incomplete lives. Consider this. In time, everything will pass, and all attachments will be lost. Loss involves suffering. Living by having is to set store by impermanent things and so to suffer loss after loss. Attachment to property and the status that goes with it isn't the way to find salvation.

However, Fromm's notion of being is fundamentally different from this. It first appears as the practice of non-attachment in the eastern religions of Hinduism, Jainism, Taoism and Buddhism. It can be found in eastern Christian monasticism and comes into modern focus with the teachings of Francis of Assisi and Ignatius of Loyola. It's also a central tenet of the Bahá'í Faith.

Being is not about having things or gaining status. Instead, it's an orientation to life in which self-renewal and development is the main focus of attention. People who live this way avoid the constant fear and inevitably of loss. They can never lose what they've never had. Being is based upon stillness. It becomes rather than begets. Those who live by being have no interest in displays of status. These are seen for what they are - short-lived and pointless shows of vanity.

The stillness of being allows the eternal or what T. S. Eliot describes as, 'now here, now always' to enter people's lives.[195] An experience of the eternal restores life to its source. Like a loving mother, the eternal is ever-present. She's ever-forgiving and is always ready to uphold those who come close to her.

Fromm's distinction between having and being can help us to understand the Quaker value of simplicity. It's recognised that people need to have things to live their lives. They need to eat, drink, dress and be sheltered. But whilst it's necessary to have things, it's unnecessary to make the getting of things the sole purpose of life. They are convinced that they can't live fulfilled lives by bread alone. They need that nourishment which arises from the depths of their being, where 'truth doth flourish as the rose.' That's why Quakers try to find a balance between having and being. Life will always test them, but their needs can be tempered with joy.

Truth

Simplicity can also refer to lives that are lived without guile and which are grounded in truth. At the trial of Jesus, Pontius Pilate asked, 'What is truth?' That's a good question and one that still exercises the minds of many postmodern thinkers. What do Quakers make of it? There are several aspects of their understanding of truth, and two of these can be mentioned here.

The first is how the term truth is commonly understood. In the Ten Commandments, we find, 'Thou shalt not bear false witness against thy neighbour.' We are commanded not to say one thing and mean another. For a variety of reasons, that's easier said than done. Sometimes, people tell their loved ones 'white lies' because the truth might be too much to bear. And sometimes, people honestly believe they are telling the truth when, in fact, they are not. There are occasions too when it isn't clear what the truth of the matter is. Nevertheless, despite these difficulties, Quakers do what they can to be truthful.

However, being truthful doesn't mean being blunt. In Paul's letter to the Ephesians, he advises that they speak the truth with love.[196] There are ways of being truthful. Following Paul's advice, Quakers try to tell the truth lovingly. It can be done. It just requires sensitivity and discernment to do it with genuine intent.

Trying to tell the truth and being as honest as possible can bring results. Early Quakers came to be known as honest people. That reputation helped them to become trusted in business and commerce. It led to them becoming successful in providing financial services. Quakers founded Barclays Bank, Friends Provident and Lloyds Bank (none of which now have any Quaker connections) and were prosperous ventures.

Indeed, aspects of Quakers' attitude to truth has caught the popular imagination. Their much-loved expression 'speaking truth unto power' crops up in everyday conversations. The phrase carries with it the Quaker commitment to the equality of all. To those in positions of power, the truth might be inconvenient. It's truth, nevertheless, and it should be spoken firmly and without fear or malice.

Speaking truth unto power has also landed Quakers in trouble. In the early days, they refused to swear oaths of allegiance to the king. They also refused to swear oaths when standing as witnesses in courts of law. In both cases, they cited the Biblical injunction to 'swear not.' They refused to swear an oath in courts of law because committing to tell the truth inside a court implies that Quakers might not do so outside of it. It suggested a double standard of truthfulness. Quakers believed that inside or outside, there can only be one level of truth. In 1695, after years of being punished for their refusal to swear, Parliament came up with a compromise. Quakers were allowed to make a *solemn affirmation* before the court that they would continue to declare the truth. To this day, the option of affirming still applies to Quakers. Indeed, the act of affirming was favoured by the former Home Secretary, Sajid Javid. He wanted it to replace what he felt was the archaic practice of oath-taking in courts of law when British society contained diverse religious and secular peoples.

Later in their history, Quakers spoke truth unto power when they were required by law to enlist in the armed forces and fight for their countries. They refused to comply. In the 1980s, Quakers in Britain and in the United States spoke truth unto power when they declared it was wrong to use tax-payers money to finance the production of military weapons and then use these to wage war. War, and the ruination of other peoples' lives, was immoral. For a time, some Quakers refused to pay a portion of their income tax for military purposes and went to great lengths through the courts to test their right to do so.

The Quaker understanding of truth has another meaning, and this is fundamental to the Quaker way of life. We've seen how Quakers worship in gathered silence. In that silence, they sense an opening between worlds and are drawn into an awareness of being close to God. Being close to God involves a responsibility. They have to listen. They wait upon the inner voice, the promptings of love which they believe to be the direct leadings of God's will. This involves discernment, a recognition of the difference between everyday mental chatter and that which is given by the spirit. There is no practical way of doing this. It isn't something that can be taught and learned. It arises in stilled minds in its own way. But when it's heard, it's clear and compelling, like the remembered voice of a loved one. These leadings are cues for action. They're never acted upon impulsively or without consideration. They're shared with others and returned to silence. There they are tended reverentially as seeds of faith. What comes forth is what Quakers call the truth.

Some people might find that fanciful, but it isn't. Sometimes the truth goes unnoticed. It's personal, but that doesn't mean it's without effect. Its influence can be life-changing. It might move someone to do something or not do something, and this might have major consequences in their lives. At other times, its effects are pivotal. They change the course of history. Truth has been the source of so much of worth in the modern world. Take, for example, the work of Seebohm Rowntree, the York Quaker. In the late nineteenth and early twentieth centuries, Rowntree worked for his family's chocolate manufacturing business. Rowntree had heard about Charles Booth's studies of poverty in London. But it was in meetings for worship where he was led by the spirit to conduct a series of social scientific surveys on poverty in York. These pioneering studies demonstrated that poverty wasn't caused by idleness or the feckless habits of the poor, as had been supposed.

13. Seebohm Rowntree with Lloyd George, May 1920

It was caused by old age, unemployment and illness, and wages that were insufficient to meet the basic costs of staying alive and well. Rowntree's work inspired a generation of politicians, including David Lloyd George, who was then the President of the Board of Trade. Rowntree and Lloyd George became close friends. Their friendship was productive. It was the creative force behind the Liberal Reforms of the early twentieth century. It presided over the birth of the modern welfare state.

What began with an experience of the leadings of the spirit in meetings for worship was to change the world beyond recognition. The reforms brought pensions for the over seventies, national health insurance, sickness benefit, workers' compensation for injuries sustained at work, family tax relief, free medical treatment for school children, a probation service as an alternative to youth imprisonment and free school meals for poor children. That's not fancy; it's the difference between bread and a borrowed shroud.

The early Quakers used to call themselves Friends of the Truth. I haven't heard modern Quakers describe themselves in that way. It wouldn't be advisable these days; it would probably come across as thoughtless, hollow or pretentious. But if modern Quakers did choose to call themselves that, I wouldn't shy away from it because I believe that's what they are. Quakers are Friends of Truth.

Equality, peace, love of the created world, simplicity and truth are Quaker responses to the world. Despite the economic and social injustice, religious and racial conflicts, deadening pollution, and all the gaudiness and deceptions of modern life, Quakers have remained faithful to the leadings of the inner light and are sustained by its power. How could it be otherwise? That's the Quaker way.

Notes

3. Preface

1. Irvin Yalom, *Existential Psychotherapy*, New York: Basic Books, 1980.

2. Abraham Maslow, *Toward a Psychology of Being*, New York, John Wiley & Sons, 1999, p. xlvi.

3. Ken Wilber, *Integral Psychology: Consciousness, Spirit, Psychology, Therapy*, Boulder, Colorado: Shambhala Publications Inc, 2000.

4. Jon James, *Transcendental Phenomenological Psychology: Introduction to Husserl's Psychology of Human Consciousness*, Victoria, British Columbia: Trafford Publishing, 2007.

5. Manavasi Parthasarathi, *Transcendental Psychology: Psychology Based on the Eternal Law of Reality*, Independently Published, 2014.

6. Eric Santner, *On the Psychotheology of Everyday Life: Reflections on Freud and Rosenzweig*, Chicago: University of Chicago Press, 2001.

7. Paul V. Axton, *The Psychotheology of Sin and Salvation*, Edinburgh: Bloomsbury Publishing PLC, 2015.

8. Andrew Bowie, (ed.) Friedrich Schleiermacher, *Hermeneutics and Criticism And Other Writings*, Cambridge: Cambridge University Press, 1998.

9. Rudolf Otto, *The Idea of the Holy*, trans. John Harvey, London: Oxford University Press, 1936.

10. Victor White, *God and the Unconscious*, London: Harvill Press, 1952.

11. Lorna Marsden, 'Science, Spirit and Imagination,' *Friends Quarterly*, Vol. 31. no. 7, 1999, pp. 315-320.

12. Matthew Fox, *Original Blessing*, Santa Fe, New Mexico: Bear & Company, 1983.

13. Hans Küng, *Eternal Life?*, London: Collins Publishers, 1984.

14. Paul Tillich, *The New Being*, London: SCM Press Ltd., 1956, pp. 152-160.

15. Don Cupitt, *Only Human*, London: SCM Press Ltd., 1985.

4.Prologue

16. Joseph Campbell, *The Power of Myth*, New York: Doubleday, 1988, p. 67.

17. Robert Neelly Bellah, *Beyond Belief: Essays on Religion in a Post-Traditional World*, New York: Harper & Row, 1970, pp. xx-xxi.

5. The Paradox of Being

18. Paul Tillich, *Love, Power and Justice*, London: Oxford University Press, 1954, p. 25.

19. Justin McCann, (ed.) *The Cloud of Unknowing*, London: Burns Oates, 1952, Title Page.

20. Mother Julian, *Revelations of Divine Love*, London: Hodder & Stoughton, 1987, p. 147.

21. Hugh I'Anson Fausset, *Fruits of Silence: Studies in the Art of Being*, London: Abelard-Schuman, 1963, p. 123.

22. Carl Gustav Jung, *Memories, Dreams, Reflections*, London: Fontana Press, 1995, p. 65.

23. Brother Lawrence, *The Practice of the Presence of God*, Grand Rapids: Spire Books, 2003, p. 31.

24. Brother Lawrence, *The Practice of the Presence of God*, Grand Rapids: Spire Books, 2003, p. 45.

25. Brother Lawrence, *The Practice of the Presence of God*, Grand Rapids: Spire Books, 2003, p. 37.

26. Mervin Mayer, trans, *The Gospel of Thomas*, New York: HarperCollins, 1992, Saying 101, p. 105.

27. Thomas Merton, *Thoughts in Solitude*, London: Burns & Oates, 1958, p. 93.

6. The Eternal Embrace

28. Richard Gregg, *Self-transcendence*, London: Gollancz, 1956, pp. 61-62.

29. Paul Tillich, *Selected Writings*, London: Collins, 1987, p. 330.

30. *John* 17:21.

31. Joseph Campbell, *The Power of Myth*, New York: Doubleday, 1988, pp. 226-228.

32. *Revelations* 1:8.

33. John Nickalls, (ed.) *The Journal of George Fox*, London: Cambridge University Press, 1952, pp. 673-674 and 65-66.

34. A. Neave Brayshaw, *The Personality of George Fox*, London: Allenson & Co. Ltd., n.d. p. 88.

7. The Ribbon of Time

35. Halcyon Backhouse, *Meister Eckhart*, Sevenoaks: Hodder & Stoughton, 1992, pp. 92-93.

36. Peter D. Ouspensky, *The Symbolism of the Tarot*, London: Universal Books, 1985. p. 52.

37. Joseph Campbell, *The Power of Myth*, New York: Doubleday, 1988, p. 202.

38. Michael A. Dummett and Anthony Flew, 'Can An Effect Precede Its Cause?,' *Proceedings of the Aristotelian Society*, Supplementary vol. xxviii, 1954, pp. 27-62.

39. Mary Hesse, *Forces and Fields*, New York: Philosophical Library, 2008.

40. John L. Mackie, *The Cement of the Universe*, Oxford: Oxford University Press, 1974.

41. Rupert Sheldrake, *A New Science of Life*, London: Paladin, 1983.

42. Sean Carroll, *From Eternity to Here*, London: Oneworld Publications, 2010.

43. Lorna Marsden, *The Descent of the God*, York: Sessions Book Trust, 1999, pp. 42-50.

8. The Secret of the Rowan Cross

44. See Géza Róheim, *Animism, Magic, and the Divine King*. London: Kegan Paul, Trench, Trubner Co. Ltd., 1930 p. 101. and Diane Purkiss, *Troublesome Things: A History of Fairies and Fairy Stories*, London: Penguin Books, 2001, p. 16.

45. Tom C. Lethbridge, *Gogmagog: The Buried Gods*, London: Book Club Associates, 1957, p. 126.

46. New English Bible, *Mark* 14:34-36.

9. Life and Death

47. *Genesis* 3:3.

48. *Romans* 6:23.

49. James Strachey, (ed.) Sigmund Freud, *Beyond the Pleasure Principle*, London: Hogarth Press, 1974, p. 32.

50. Carl Gustav Jung, 'The Stages of Life,' *C.G. Jung The Collected Works*, trans. R.F.C. Hull, London: Routledge & Kegan Paul, 1987, Vol. 8, p. 482.

51. Ken Wilber, 'The Great Chain of Being,' in Roger Walsh and Frances Vaughan, (eds.) *Paths Beyond Ego*, New York: Jeremy P. Tarcher, 1993, pp. 214-222.

52. Grevel Lindop, (ed.) Robert Graves, *The White Goddess*, Manchester: Carcanet, 1997, *passim*.

53. Carl Gustav Jung, *C.G. Jung The Collected Works*, trans. R.F.C. Hull, London: Routledge & Kegan Paul, 1987, Vol. 5, p. 158.

54. Friedrich Nietzsche, *Thus Spoke Zarathustra*, trans. R. J. Hollingdale, Harmondsworth, Middlesex: Penguin Books Ltd., 1966.

55. See for example, Károly Kerényi, *Dionysos: Archetypal Image of Indestructable Life*, trans. Ralph Manheim, London: Routlege & Kegan Paul, 1976, pp. xxxi-xxxvii.

56. C. S. Lewis, *Beyond Personality*, London: Geoffrey Bles, 1945, p. 14.

10. Breaking the Chains

57. See Pierre Teilhard de Chardin, *The Vision of the Past*, London: Collins, 1966, p. 180.

58. *Genesis* 3:8.

59. Hippolytus *Refutation*, I, ii.

60. William Keith Chambers Guthrie, *The Greek Philosophers*, London: Methuen, 1978, p. 36.

61. Alfred North Whitehead, *Process and Reality: An Essay on Cosmology*, New York: Free Press, 1979, p. 39.

62. Calvin J. Roetzel, *The Letters of Paul*, 5th ed., Louisville, Kentucky: Westminster John Knox Press, 2009, pp. 19-57.

63. Aaron Ridley and Judith Norman, (eds.) Friedrich Nietzsche, *The Anti-Christ, Ecce Homo, Twilight of the Idols and other Writings*, Cambridge: Cambridge University Press, 2005, p. 38.

64. Aaron Ridley and Judith Norman, (eds.) Friedrich Nietzsche, *The Anti-Christ, Ecce Homo, Twilight of the Idols and other Writings*, Cambridge: Cambridge University Press, 1987, p. 37.

65. Calvin J. Roetzel, *The Letters of Paul*, 5th ed., Louisville, Kentucky: Westminster John Knox Press, 2009, *passim*.

66. Elaine Pagels, *The Origin of Satan*, London: Allen Lane, The Penguin Press, 1995, p. 151.

67. Ralph Waldo Emerson, *Journal*, December 21st, 1823.

68. Charles Dickens, *A Christmas Carol*, London: Oldhams Press, nd. Stave One, p. 26.

69. Peter Berger and Thomas Luckmann, *The Social Construction of Reality*, London: The Penguin Press, 1967, p. 17.

70. Thomas Green, *Preparation for Worship*, London: Quaker Home Service, 1983, p. 5.

71. Thomas Robinson, *Heraclitus: Fragments*, Toronto: Phoenix Supplementary Paperback, 1987, p. 61.

72. Joseph Campbell, *The Power of Myth*, New York: Doubleday, 1988, p. 67.

73. Joseph Campbell, *The Power of Myth*, New York: Doubleday, 1988, p. 66.

74. Evelyn Underhill, *Mysticism*, London: Methuen & Co Ltd., 1945, p. 38.

75. Franz Pfeiffer, *The Sermons and Collations of Meister Eckhart*, Whitefish, Montana, 1992, p. 4.

76. Isaac Penington, *Letters of Isaac Penington*, 2nd ed., Philadelphia: Friends' Bookstore, nd., p. 115.

77. *Galatians* 3:28.

78. Thomas Green, *Preparation for Worship*, London: Quaker Home Service, 1983, p. 4.

79. Brother Lawrence, *The Practice of the Presence of God*, Grand Rapids: Spire Books, 2003, p. 79.

80. Brother Lawrence, *The Practice of the Presence of God*, Grand Rapids: Spire Books, 2003, pp. 89-90.

81. 1 *Corinthians* 12:8.

11. *The Powers of Light and Darkness*

82. See for example, Stephan A. Hoeller, *Gnosticism: New Light on the Ancient Tradition of Inner Knowing*, Wheaton: Illinois, 2002, p. 57. Timothy Freke & Peter Gandy, *The Laughing Jesus*, Ropley, Hants: O Books, 2006, p. 151. and Lena Einhorn, *The Jesus Mystery*, Guilford, Connecticut: The Lyons Press, 2007, p. 85.

83. *Thessalonians*, 5:5.

84. *Romans*, 13:12.

85. *John*, 3:18-19.

86. For several years, Augustine, 'Father of the Church,' was a follower of Manichaeism and although he was eventually to reject it, in is seminal text, *Confessions*, there are aspects of theology that bear unmistakable Manichean characteristics.

87. Samuel N. C. Lieu, *Manichaeism*, Manchester: Manchester University Press, 1999, p. 8.

88. Joseph Campbell, *The Power of Myth*, New York: Doubleday, 1988, p. 21.

89. John Robinson, *Honest to God*, London: SCM Press Ltd., 1963.

90. Kenneth Clark, *Civilisation*, London: BBC & John Murray, 1973, p. 212.

91. See John Morris, 'Descartes's Natural Light,' in Georges Moyal, *René Descartes: Critical Assessments*, Vol. 1, London: Routledge, 1991, pp. 413-432.

92. See for example, Erwin Stengle, *Suicide and Attempted Suicide*, London: MacGibbon & Kee, 1965, pp. 34-35. and Benard V. Geoffroy and Frank Bellivier, 'Seasons, Circadian Rhythms, Sleep and Suicidal Behaviours Vulnerability,' *L'Encephale*, 41, (4 Suppl 1): S 29-337, 2015.

93. John Keats, *Lamia II*, Lines 234-237.

94. Alan Jacobs, 'The Gospel of Philip,' in *The Essential Gnostic Gospels*, London: Watkins Publishing, 2006, p. 56.

95. Claude Levi-Strauss, *The Naked Man*, London: Jonathan Cape, 1981, p.349.

96. Edmund Spencer, *The Faerie Queene*, Book 1, Canto 1, Line 122.

97. Michael Doran, (ed.) *Conversations with Cézanne*, Berkeley: University of California Press, 2001, p. 196.

98. Kahlil Gibran, *The Prophet*, London: Wordsworth Classics, 1996, p. 16.

99. James Joyce, *Portrait of the Artist as a Young Man*, London: Wordsworth Classics, 1992, p. 170.

100. Walt Whitman, 'The Prayer of Columbus,' *Complete Poetry & Selected Prose and Letters*, London: The Nonesuch Press, 1939, p. 383.

101. John O'Donohue, *Anam Cara*, London: Bantam Press, 1997, p. 92.

102. Jeanne Guyon, *The Spiritual Adventure*, Gardiner, Maine: Christian Books, 1985, p. 58.

12. *Flowers of Light*

103. Dante Gabriel Rossetti, *The Blessed Damozel*, Edinburgh: R. Grant & Son, 1903, p. 1.

104. See for example, the illustration in Carl Jung, *Psychology and Alchemy*, London: Routledge, 1993, p. 213.

105. Marina Warner, *Alone of All Her Sex* , London: Picador, 1990.

106. Janet & Stewart Farrar, *The Witches' Goddess: the Feminine Principle of Divinity*, London: Hale, 1987, p. 175.

107. See for example, 'The Madonna with the Iris' by Albrecht Dürer [c1500]. Prime examples of the Virgin crowned with fleurs-de-lis can be found in the Church of St Martin-on-the Hill, Scarborough, in Yorkshire.

108. Edward Burnett Tylor, *Primitive Culture: Researches into the Development of Mythology, Philosophy, Religion, Art and Custom*, London: J. Murray, 1971.

109. See for example, Sigmund Freud, *Totem and Taboo*, London: Routledge & Kegan Paul, 1961.

110. Carl Gustav Jung, *The Integration of the Personality*, London: Kegan Paul, Trench, Trubner & Co Ltd., 1944, pp. 205-281.

111. Jean Cooper, *Symbolism*, Wellingborough: The Aquarian Press, 1982, p.83.

112. D. H. Lawrence, 'Scent of Irises,' *Love Poems*, London: Studio Vista, 1965, p. 18.

113. See for example, Alby Stone, 'A Threefold Cosmos,' *At the Edge*, No 5, Loughborough, 1997, pp. 7-12.

114. Marie-Louise von Franz, *Number and Time*, London: Rider & Company, 1974, p. 102.

115. Aristotle, *On the Heavens*, Charleston: BiblioLife, 2009, p. 9.

116. Aristotle, *On the Heavens*, Charleston: BiblioLife, 2009, p 9.

117. Joseph Campbell, *The Inner Reaches of Outer Space*, California: New World Library, 2002, p. 11.

118. William Shakespeare, *Macbeth* (1.iii. 36-37).

119. Marina Warner, *Alone of All Her Sex*, London: Picador, 1990, p. 266.

120. Richard Mabey, *Flora Britannica*, London: Sinclair-Stevenson, 1996, p. 434.

121. Daniel C. Matt, *The Essential Kabbalah*, New York: Harper San Francisco, 1996, p.110.

13. *Time and Eternity*

122. Ursula Fleming, (ed.) *Meister Eckhart: The Man From Whom God Hid Nothing*, Leominster: Gracewing, 1995, pp. 67-68.

123. Ursula Fleming, (ed.) *Meister Eckhart: The Man From Whom God Hid Nothing*, Leominster: Gracewing, 1995, pp. 65-66.

124. Laurent Olivier, 'The Past of the Present: Archaeological Memory and Time,' *Archaeological Dialogues*, 10(2), pp. 204-213.

125. Roger Sapsford, Arthur Still, Margaret Wetherell, Dorothy Meill and Richard Stevens (eds.) *Theory and Social Psychology*, London: Sage Publications in association with the Open University, 1998, *passim.*

126. James Strachey, (ed.) Sigmund Freud, *Beyond the Pleasure Principle*, London: The Hogarth Press, 1974.

127. See Albert Cook Outler, (ed.) *Augustine: Confessions and Enchiridion*, Louisville, Kentucky: Westminster John Knox Press, 1955. Boethius, *The Consolation of Philosophy*, Book V, Prosa 6, London: Penguin Classics, 1999. and C. S. Lewis, *Beyond Personality*, London: Geoffrey Bles: The Centenary Press, 1945, pp. 19-23.

128. James Strachey, (ed.) Sigmund Freud, *Beyond the Pleasure Principle*, London: The Hogarth Press, 1974, p. 22.

129. Joseph Cambell, *The Power of Myth*, New York: Doubleday, 1988, *passim.*

130. M. K. Bradby, *Psychoanalysis*, London Hodder & Stoughton, 1919, pp. 28-41.

131. Robert Ornstein,*The Psychology of Consciousness*, London: Jonathan Cape, 1975, p. 76.

132. See for example,Cristina Bacchilega, *Postmodern Fairy Tales*, Philadelphia: University of Pennsylvalia Press, 1997. and Alister McGrath, *The Twilight of Atheism: The Rise and Fall of Disbelief in the Modern World*, London: Rider, 2004.

133. See for example, Erich Fromm, *The Forgotten Language*, New York: Grove Press, 1951. Julius Heuscher, *A Psychiatric Study of Myths and Fairy Tales*, Springfield: Charles C. Thomas, 1974. and Peter O'Connor, *Beyond the Mist: Reflections on Irish Mythology*, London: Victor Gollancz, 2000.

134. Henry Habberley Price, *Essays in the Philosophy of Religion*, London: Oxford University Press, 1972.

135. Joseph Cambell, *The Power of Myth*, New York: Doubleday, 1988, p. 67.

136. Walter Benjamin, *Illuminations: Essays and Reflections*, trans. Hannah Arendt, New York: Harcourt, Brace Jovanovich. 1968, p. 253, XIII.

137. Joseph Campbell, *The Power of Myth*, New York: Doubleday, 1988, *passim*.

138. Richard Gregg, *Self-transcendence*, London: Gollancz, pp. 61-62.

139. Robert Ornstein, *The Psychology of Consciousness*, London: Jonathan Cape, 1975, pp. 103-141.

140. Mircea Eliade, *The Sacred and the Profane*, San Diego: Harcourt Inc. 1961, p. 71.

141. Paul Tillich, *The Eternal Now*, SCM Press Ltd., 1963, p. 76.

142. William Blake, *The Poetical Works*, 'Jerusalem,' F 15, 11, line 8, London: Oxford University Press, 1908.

143. Lorna Marsden, *From the Frontier*, Sutton, Surrey: The Open Letter Movement, 1981, p. 16.

144. Lorna Marsden, *From the Frontier*, Sutton, Surrey: The Open Letter Movement, 1981, p. 24.

145. Jean-Pierre, de Caussade, *Abandonment to Divine Providence*, trans. E.L. Strickland, New York: Grove Press, 2007.

146. Sigmund Freud, *The Interpretation of Dreams*, London: George Allen & Unwin, 1971.

147. The numerology of these events is remarkable. The young man's experience was in 1971 ie $1 + 9 + 7 + 1 = 18$ and $1 + 8 = 9$. His daughter's experience was in 2007 ie $2 + 0 + 0 + 7 = 9$. The period

between the events was 36 years ie 3 + 6 = 9. In contemporary western numerology, the number 9 represents beginnings and endings, that is to say, it represents the possibility of new life. This illustration was first used at a conference in The Elphinstone Institute in Aberdeen in the summer of 2013. The author was somewhat bemused to find that on the way to the conference the train to Aberdeen left from Platform 9 in York station.

148. John Ruskin, *Modern Painters*, Vol. 3, Part 4, Chapter 14, London: Smith, Elder & Co., 1856.

Appendix

A Transpersonal Psychology

149. Carl Rogers, 'A Theory of Therapy, Personality and Interpersonal Relationships, as Developed in the Client-centred Framework,' in Sigmund Koch (ed.) *Psychology: A Study of Science*, New York: McGraw-Hill, 1959, p. 192.

150. Carl Rogers, *Client-Centred Therapy: Its Current Practice, Implications and Theory*, London: Constable, 1951, p. 487.

151. Friedrich Nietzsche, *Thus Spoke Zarathustra*, trans. R. J. Hollingdale, Harmondsworth, Middlesex: Penguin Books Ltd., 1966.

152. Dennis H. Wrong, *Skeptical Sociology*, London: Heinemann, 1977, pp. 31-54.

153. Dennis H. Wrong, *Skeptical Sociology*, London: Heinemann, 1977, pp. 1-2.

154. Eugene T. Gendlin, *Focusing*, London: Rider, 2003.

155. See for example, Jonathan D. Raskin, 'Evolutionary Constructivism and Humanistic Psychology,' *Journal of Theoretical and Philosophical Psychology*, Vol. 32, No 2, 2012, pp. 119-133. and Eleanor Criswell, *Biofeedback and Somatics: Toward Personal Evolution*, Novato, California: Freeperson Press, 1995.

156. Michael Wallach and Lise Wallach, *Psychology's Sanction for Selfishness: Error of Egoism in Theory and Therapy*, New York: W. H. Freeman & Co, 1983.

157. Rollo May, 'The Problem of Evil: An Open Letter To Carl Rogers,' *Journal of Humanistic Psychology*, Vol. 22, No 3, 1986, pp. 10-21.

158. Ian Parker, *Psychology After Deconstruction*, Milton, Abingdon: Taylor & Francis, 2014.

159. Isaac Prilleltcnsky, 'Humanistic Psychology, Human Welfare and the Social Order,' *Journal of Mind and Behaviour,* Vol. 13, No 4, 1992, pp. 315-327.

160. Robert Shaw and Karen Colmore, 'Humanistic Psychology as Ideology: An Analysis of Maslow's Contradictions,' *Journal of Humanistic Psychology*, Vol. 28, Issue 3, 1988, pp. 51-74.

161. Erich Lindemann, *Crisis Intervention*, Lanham, Maryland: Jason Aronson Inc., 1977. and Gerald Caplan, *Support Systems and Mental Health*, New York: Springer, 1974.

162. Anthony J. Sutich, 'On The Emergence of the Transpersonal Psychology Orientation: A Personal Account,' *Journal of Transpersonal Psychology*, Vol. 8, No 1, 1976, pp. 5-19.

163. Anthony J. Sutich, 'On The Emergence of the Transpersonal Psychology Orientation: A Personal Account' *Journal of Transpersonal Psychology*, Vol. 8, No 1, 1976, p. 7.

164. Abraham Maslow, *The Psychology of Science: A Reconnaissance*, Nevada City, California: Gateway, 1969.

165. Abraham Maslow, *The Farther Reaches of Human Nature*, New York: Viking, 1971, p. 183.

166. Abraham Maslow, *The Farther Reaches of Human Nature*, New York: Viking, 1971, p. 256.

167. Anthony J. Sutich, 'On The Emergence of the Transpersonal Psychology Orientation: A Personal Account,' *Journal of Transpersonal Psychology*, Vol. 8, No 1, 1976, pp. 13-14.

168. Ken Wilber, *Integral Psychology: Consciousness, Spirit, Psychology, Therapy*, Boulder, Colorado: Shambhala Publications Inc., 2000.

169. Michael Daniels, *Shadow Self & Spirit: Essays in Transpersonal Psychology*, Exeter: Imprint Academic, 2005, p. 93.

170. Albert Ellis, 'Dangers of Transpersonal Psychology: A Reply to Wilber,' *Journal of Counseling & Development*, Vol. 67, Issue 6, 1989, p. 336.

171. See for example, Rollo May, Stanley Krippner and Jacqueline Doyle, 'The Role of Transpersonal Psychology in Psychology as a Whole: A Discussion,' *The Humanistic Psychologist*, Vol. 20 (2-3) 1992, pp. 307-317. and Mark Schroll, John Rowan and Oliver Robinson, 'Clearing Up Rollo May's View of Transpersonal Psychology and Acknowledging May as an Early Supporter of Ecopsychology,' *International Journal of Transpersonal Studies*, Vol. 30, Issue 1-2, 2011, pp. 120-136.

172. Eugene Taylor, 'Transpersonal Psychology: Its Several Virtues,' *The Humanistic Psychologist*, Vol. 20, (2-3) 1992, pp. 285-300.

173. Kirk J. Schneider, 'The Deified Self: A 'Centaur' Response to Wilber and the Transpersonal Movement,' *Journal of Humanistic Psychology*, Vol. 27, No 2, 1987, p. 199.

B. The Quaker Way

174. Vernon Noble, *The Man in Leather Breaches*, London: Elek Books, 1953, pp. 49-50.

175. Beginning with the Act of Uniformity 1662.

176. John O'Donohue, *Anam Cara*, London: Bantam Press, 1997, p. 99.

177. *Romans* 12:2.

178. Karen Horney, *Neurosis and Human Growth: The Struggle for Self-Realization*, New York: W. W. Norton & Co Inc., 1991, p. 64.

179. James Nayler, *A True Discoverie of Faith, and A Brief Manifestation of the Ground upon which we stand, to those who desire to know it.* 1655, p. 11.

180. *Quaker Faith & Practice*, 2nd ed., London: The Yearly Meeting of the Religious Society of Friends (Quakers) Britain, 1999.

181. https://quaker.org

182. George Macaulay Trevelyan, *English Social History*, London: Longmans, 1944, p. 267.

183. John Nickalls, (ed.) *The Journal of George Fox*, London: Cambridge University Press, 1952, p. 197.

184. https://www.peacemuseum.org.uk

185. William Penn, *Some Fruits of Solitude*, Richmond: Indiana: Friends United Press, 2007, p. 16.

186. Martin Buber, *I and Thou*, London: Bloomsbury Academic, 2004.

187. Murray Bodo, trans. *Through the Year With Francis of Assisi*, London: Fount Paperbacks, 1988, p. 169.

188. Murray Bodo, trans. *Through the Year With Francis of Assisi*, London: Fount Paperbacks, 1988, p. 41.

189. Murray Bodo, trans. *Through the Year With Francis of Assisi*, London: Fount Paperbacks, 1988, p. 185.

190. Margaret Hebblethwaite, *Way of St Ignatius: Finding God in All Things*, London: HarperCollins, 1987, p. 211.

191. Guy Ragland Phillips, *The Unpolluted God*, Pocklington: Northern Lights, 1987, p. 246.

192. T. S. Eliot, 'Little Gidding,' in Bernard Berganzi, (ed.) *Four Quartets*, London: Palgrave, 1969.

193. *Quaker Faith & Practice*, 2nd ed., London: The Yearly Meeting of the Religious Society of Friends (Quakers) Britain, 1999, Advices and Queries, 1.02, 42.

194. Erich Fromm, *To Have or to Be?*, London: Abacus, Sphere Books Ltd., 1979, *passim*.

195. T. S. Eliot, 'Little Gidding,' in Bernard Berganzi, (ed.) *Four Quartets*, London: Palgrave, 1969.

196. *Ephesians* 4:15.

Name Index

Subject Index

A

Agape, 144
Altered states of consciousness, xv, 123, 124-125, 139, 159
American Declaration of Independence, 146
American dream, 146
Angelus, 113
Anomie, 72
Anti-Enlightenment, 132, 135, 140, 141-144
Anxiety, xi, 6, 10, 11, 20, 21, 23, 46, 54, 70, 72, 96, 154, 176
Atheists, 135, 168
Authentic life, 13, 14, 17

B

Babylonians, 59, 61, 63, 103, 110
Bahá'i Faith, 77, 168, 193
Behavioural psychology and Behaviourism, xiv, 136, 137, 140, 162
Bios, 55-57
Blood in spells, 40
Buddhists and Buddhism, xiii, xviii, 26, 139, 155, 168, 193

C

Christians and Christianity, xviii, 18, 45, 48, 49, 56, 61, 63, 65, 66, 68, 69, 79, 82, 84, 86, 110, 168, 171, 175, 181, 182, 193
Chronological snobbery, 68-69
Church of Saint Martin-on-the Hill, 207
Cinderella complex, 167, 171
Cloud of Unknowing, 17, 171
Conscious and consciousness, xiv, xv, xvii, xix, xx, 12, 18, 24, 27, 43, 44, 45, 52, 57, 66, 84, 86, 89, 93, 94, 96, 99, 110, 115, 117-123, 139, 143, 156, 157, 158, 159, 164-165, 166

D

Death, xi, 5, 9, 11, 14, 23, 25, 28, 32, 37, 45, 47-57, 60-61, 64, 65, 66, 67, 78, 82, 88, 90, 91, 129, 152, 154, 158, 176, 184, 188, 189
Death of Plato, 65
Definitions, xix-xx, 89, 119-120, 121, 123, 146, 165, 172
Depression, 5-6
Doctrine of signatures, 108
Dreams and dreaming, 35, 90, 95, 97, 99, 124, 126, 129-130, 134, 143, 146, 158

E

Empty lives, 4, 6, 7, 12-13, 70, 89
Enlightenment the, 87-90, 92, 122, 132-135, 137, 140, 141, 143, 146
Epic of Creation, 81
Epic of Gilgamesh, 105-106
Equality, 133, 145, 146, 179-181, 196, 199
Esalen Institute, 139, 155
Essenes, 83-84
Eternal return, 53
Eternal life, xviii, 9, 16, 46, 74, 78, 94, 95, 97, 113, 115, 116, 117, 123, 124, 126
Eternity, xi-xii, xvii, xix, xx, xxi, 1, 2, 8, 9, 14, 15-17, 18, 19, 21, 23, 25-32, 35, 38, 56, 57, 60, 75, 77, 97, 113, 115, 117-128, 158, 166
Existential psychology and existential psychologists, xi, xiii, xvi, 11, 12, 138

F

Friends' Theological College Kenya, 170

G

Garden of Eden, 8, 61-62, 78, 113-114
Gnostics and Gnosticism, 9, 50, 63, 65, 85, 91

218